Impactful Practices for Early Childhood Teacher Educators

Impactful Practices for Early Childhood Teacher Educators

Edited by
Christopher Meidl
Louise Ammentorp

ROWMAN & LITTLEFIELD
Lanham • Boulder • New York • London

Published by Rowman & Littlefield
An imprint of The Rowman & Littlefield Publishing Group, Inc.
4501 Forbes Boulevard, Suite 200, Lanham, Maryland 20706
www.rowman.com

6 Tinworth Street, London SE11 5AL

Copyright © 2019 by Christopher Meidl and Louise Ammentorp

All rights reserved. No part of this book may be reproduced in any form or by any electronic or mechanical means, including information storage and retrieval systems, without written permission from the publisher, except by a reviewer who may quote passages in a review.

British Library Cataloguing in Publication Information Available

Library of Congress Control Number: 2019949388

Contents

Preface: A Need for Sharing Practice ... vii

Part I: Broadening Awareness, Transforming Beliefs, and Developing Community ... 1

1. Activity Plan Simulations: Preservice Teachers Developing Skills to Interact with Exceptional Early Childhood Children in Inclusive Settings ... 3
Leslie Craigo

2. Creating Voice: Using Mock Interviews and a Parent Panel to Establish Communicative Skills in Preservice Teachers ... 17
Christopher J. Meidl and Debra Hyatt-Burkhart

3. Making Tacit Cultural Beliefs Visible in Early Childhood Teacher Education: Facilitating Video-Cued Discussions with Teacher Candidates ... 31
MinSoo Kim-Bossard

4. Toward Belonging: Immigrant Family Stories Reinform Perspectives on Family Partnerships ... 41
Rebecca J. Pruitt

5. Listening to Voices of Families as a Transformative Process ... 51
Julia Ann Williams

6. A Pattern of Practice: The Fabric of a Playful, Active Learning Community ... 63
Laurel L. Byrne

7. Professional Learning Communities from the Inside Out: Teacher Candidates' Perceptions and Experiences ... 75
Jill A. Smith

Part II: Innovation in Curriculum and Instruction — 85

8 Hydroponic Gardens as a Learning Tool with Preservice Teachers — 87
Louise Ammentorp

9 Let's Have a Mathematical Conversation: Assessing Preservice Teachers' Ability to Do Mathematics — 97
Alan Bates

10 Connecting Things in ECE Teaching and Learning: The "Six Objects Task" — 111
Alyse C. Hachey

11 Seeking to Create Tech-Savvy Teachers — 125
Lisa L. Minicozzi

12 Using Online Teacher Education Preparation as a Way to Diversify the Early Childhood Teaching Force — 137
Billi L. Bromer

Index — 147

About the Editors and Contributors — 157

Preface

A Need for Sharing Practice

The goal of this edited volume is to share ideas and examples of impactful practices useful for teacher educators in early childhood education degree programs (associate, bachelor, and graduate level) as well as teacher educators in other settings. This book intends to provide the reader with multiple examples of effective practice, including sample sources of data (i.e., artifacts, description of activities, assignment guidelines, syllabi, photos of learning and results, student work, etc.).

At a symposium presented at the Association of Teacher Educators, the Early Childhood Special Interest Group came together to discuss best practices. As Rismark and Solvberg (2011) explain, shared practice leads to inquiry, evaluative understanding, acknowledgment, and reflexivity of teaching practice. During the symposium, discussions between presenters and audience members joining in as a participatory community organically unfolded. During those discussions, it came about that a book based on "impactful practices" in which colleagues shared some of their best practices, would benefit other early childhood teacher educators.

With the intent of sharing best practice, multiple teacher educators have contributed to this edited book as a means of sharing "impactful practice" with the field. In exploring "impactful practice" the following guiding questions arose:

1. What are challenges of practice and how do teacher educators address them?
2. How do teacher educators use *impactful practice* to develop future educators in a time of hostility toward education?

3. How can this book inform the field collectively?

The following sections of this chapter establish a definition of impactful practice, the design of the chapters, and a description of the individual chapters.

DEFINING IMPACTFUL PRACTICE

Multiple authors offer various conceptual descriptions of what impactful practice might be, including expertise and knowledge organization, progressions, and skills within a community of learners. Definitions of impactful practice can be grounded in the Interstate Teacher Assessment and Support Consortium's (InTASC) discussion of the advanced understanding of teacher skills conceptualized as *progressions*. They state that the progressions "provide guidance about how practice might be improved, and outline possible professional learning experiences to bring about such improvements" (Council of Chief State School Officers, 2013, p. 10). Further, the InTASC documents emphasize impactful practice when teachers participate in the "decision-making processes that include building a shared vision and supportive culture, identifying common goals, and monitoring progress toward those goals" (p. 5).

The National Association for the Education of Young Children (NAEYC) also contributes a narrative for defining impactful practice. The 2011 NAEYC Standards for Initial and Advanced Early Childhood Professional Preparation Programs provides a framing of impactful practice: "Early childhood candidates in well-designed programs develop professional knowledge, skills and dispositions in a community of learners, making sense of readings, observations, field experiences, and group projects through their interactions with others" (NAEYC, 2011, p. 13). Finally, the argument is made that instructors must model how to "create a caring community of learners, teach to enhance development and learning, plan curriculum aligned with important learning outcomes, assess candidate growth and development related to those outcomes, and build positive relationships with students and other stakeholders" (p. 13).

While there is no specific definition of impactful practice, a general statement can be made that the authors believe that some aspect of teaching and learning they designed and facilitated in their classroom led to learning that transformed or changed the future early childhood educators under their care. Not everything a teacher or teacher educator does can be measured, and so the goal was to have instructors consider what they have decided is impactful in transforming students into teachers. The benefit of this approach is that constructs of impactful practice can be conceptualized and applied in multiple contexts for various coursework.

CHAPTER OUTLINE

The twelve chapters in this book intend to provide examples of current practice that various early childhood teacher educators have found the most impactful. The intent is to create a space for sharing how and what a community of early childhood educators value in regard to instructional practice. The examples of instructional practice allow individuals in higher education, childcare centers, school administrators, or teachers to explore, replicate, or adapt them for course design or professional development. The chapters in the book are grouped into two themes: Broadening Awareness, Transforming Beliefs, and Developing Community; and Innovation in Curriculum and Instruction.

Broadening Awareness, Transforming Beliefs, and Developing Community

Leslie Craigo provides a narrative about an assignment in an exceptionalities class. Preservice teachers can use what they have learned about exceptional children to create activities that are engaging and culturally responsive, and that address the specific needs of individual children with exceptionalities.

Christopher J. Meidl and Debra Hyatt-Burkhart outline learning designed to help future teachers develop voice and empowerment through a parent panel and a pseudo-conference. This learning activity was developed as a formative, performance-based learning assignment in which the aspiring teachers listen to parents' experiences in schools and with teachers, and participate in a simulated conference.

MinSoo Kim-Bossard discusses an in-class activity aimed at raising cultural awareness for teacher candidates who may or may not have cross-cultural experiences. The activity introduced in this chapter is built on the premise that it is necessary for all teachers to be aware of their cultural positioning in order to make culturally sensitive instructional decisions that promote diversity and inclusion.

Rebecca J. Pruitt utilizes assignments meant to facilitate teacher candidates' reflections related to their worldviews and those of others. This chapter explains an activity used to help students analyze curriculum for bias, create antibias curriculum, understand critical pedagogy in context, and critique traditional parent involvement and teaming approaches to develop strengths-based, value-added, collaborative approaches.

Julia Ann Williams explains how transformative experiences are integral to the development of early childhood educators in a global society. The author provides class assignments and activities designed to create a multivoiced approach where preservice teachers, teacher educators, and parents work and listen to each other. The multivoiced approach is intended to allow preservice teachers to understand and work with children and families of diverse populations.

Laurel L. Byrne explains components of intentional planning to establish a learning community environment designed to foster positive relationships and rich, meaningful learning experiences that promote the overall growth and development of early childhood teacher candidates. The chapter provides readers with a look at the creation of a learning community culture that supports engaged and playful pedagogy through inquiry, exploration, and discovery.

Jill A. Smith focuses on how effective participation within collaborative learning teams helps bridge the transition from teacher education programs to the actual teaching profession. This course requires candidates to collectively develop an integrated study (thematic unit), design cross-disciplinary lesson plans related to the thematic unit, complete a field experience in a public school classroom, implement lessons, reflect on their experiences in the classroom, and complete team presentations on learning theorists and community-based educational programs.

Innovation in Curriculum and Instruction

Louise Ammentorp describes ways to use vertical hydroponic gardens as a learning tool with preservice teachers. She discusses the basics and benefits of hydroponic gardening, and strategies for using the gardens to connect preservice teachers to nature and teach a variety of topics, including lesson planning and instruction, social and emotional learning (SEL) competences, inquiry and questioning, and food access and equity.

Alan Bates implements a pedagogical approach to assessing preservice teachers' understanding of mathematics. Breaking from traditional written assessments, Bates innovatively presents an oral, one-on-one final where students are asked to teach the instructor using various math standards as described in the Common Core.

Alyse C. Hachey describes the implementation of a teaching activity that can be utilized during early childhood education (ECE) teacher preparation or professional development, dubbed by the author the "Six Objects Task." In using the "Six Objects Task" as a multilayered lesson in ECE teaching *and* learning, Hachey has participants use six common objects, individually and in various configurations of collaborative teams, for an iterative, open-ended constructive design project presented by the teacher trainer.

Lisa L. Minicozzi explains how new technologies are exerting a transformative effect in many areas of education. This chapter describes how one university professor routinely integrates iPad technology within the context of a methodology course as a means to develop candidates' skills, expertise, and teaching approaches to meet the needs of the twenty-first-century learner.

Billi L. Bromer offers a look into a unique program intended to help adults unable to enroll in traditional college degree programs because of employment, family, or other reasons to attain a degree and teacher licensure through an online undergraduate teacher education program. The chapter describes the fully online educator preparation program that uses the Canvas learning management system as a virtual classroom and leads to Georgia teacher licensure.

BIBLIOGRAPHY

Association of Teacher Educators. (2003). ATE mission. Retrieved from http://www.ate1.org/pubs/ATEs_Vision_Missio.cfm

Council of Chief State School Officers, Interstate Teacher Assessment and Support Consortium. (2013). *InTASC model core teaching standards and learning progressions for teachers 1.0: A resource for ongoing teacher development*. Washington, DC.

National Association for the Education of Young Children (NAEYC). (2011). *NAEYC standards for initial and advanced early childhood professional preparation programs*.

Rismark, Marit, & Solvberg, Astrid M. (2011). Knowledge sharing in schools: A key to developing professional learning communities. *World Journal of Education, 1*(2), 150–160.

Part I

Broadening Awareness, Transforming Beliefs, and Developing Community

Chapter One

Activity Plan Simulations

*Preservice Teachers Developing Skills to
Interact with Exceptional Early Childhood Children in
Inclusive Settings*

Leslie Craigo

Children with exceptionalities are increasingly being educated in inclusive, general education settings rather than self-contained special education classrooms (NAEYC, 2009). While there are related service professionals (i.e., speech therapists, occupational therapists, school psychologists, and special education teachers) who provide support to exceptional children in these inclusive settings, it is usually the general education classroom teacher who supplies the majority of the daily activities and learning experiences for all children. Therefore, preservice teachers need to develop competency in providing high-quality education to a variety of students (Baker-Ericzén, Garnand Muggenborg, & Shea, 2009).

Children generally develop according to an expected set of milestones. When development is significantly different than age expectation, children may exhibit characteristics of disability, impairment, giftedness, and/or atypical development. The terminology used for children who are identified as being significantly different from the norm has changed over time. Currently, one of the most inclusive terms is *exceptional children*; this term includes children at risk; children with disabilities, disorders, and impairments; the gifted and talented; and children with atypical development (Heward, 2013).

While some preservice teachers have experience with exceptional children, that experience may be personal and not professional. Many preservice teachers have limited experience—personally or professionally—with exceptional children. Preservice teacher perceptions of disability and exceptionality vary significantly based on frameworks such as a deficit lens, miraculous ("they can do anything") lens, and, with appropriate support, a children "can learn" lens. Without prior experience with exceptionality, and without a strengths-based realistic framework, providing appropriate educational experiences for exceptional children can be challenging for preservice teachers (Bialka, 2015).

A strengths-based framework focuses on what children with exceptionalities can do rather than what they cannot do. When preservice teachers focus on the strengths of their students, they can use those strengths to provide support with tasks that are challenging for their students. For example, if a student with learning disabilities struggles with math but excels at drawing, then a teacher would use the student's strength in drawing to help that student solve math problems. This strengths-based focus was particularly useful for a second grader who was struggling to use number lines or the part/part/whole methodology for basic computations. However, this child loved to draw, so when solving word problems with addition and subtraction, rather than use one of the above methods, the child was encouraged to draw. The following is an example problem: Marisa, Jose, and Lee were making a fruit salad. Marisa added five slices of banana, Jose added eight slices of orange, and Lee added 10 strawberries. How many pieces of fruit were added in all? Who added the most pieces? If John came along and took out three berries, one banana slice, and two orange slices, how many pieces of fruit would be left?

These steps were presented one at a time, and most children were able to solve the problem using a number line or the part/part/whole method. The child who struggled with math but loved to draw was able to draw pictures for each step in the problem. For the subtraction, he drew a mouth with teeth around each piece that John took out of the salad, and counted the pieces that did not have a mouth around them.

A COURSE IN FOUNDATIONS AND PEDAGOGY FOR EXCEPTIONAL CHILDREN

This chapter describes an impactful practice in an educational foundations and pedagogy for an exceptional child survey course at a community college. This is one of the last courses that students take in a seven-course, early childhood educational sequence. Students also take general education requirements and then transfer to a four-year college or work as assistant teachers. The college is located in a large urban area and is part of a citywide university system.

This course requires thirty hours of fieldwork in an inclusive setting or a self-contained classroom. Most preservice teachers complete the fieldwork in inclusive settings. The fieldwork is unsupervised, and preservice teachers locate their own placements. They frequently choose sites in which they have done supervised fieldwork. The major goals of fieldwork are as follows:

1. observation of assessment and implementation of strategies that teachers use to support exceptional children,
2. recognition of adaptations of materials and procedures that support exceptional children,
3. understanding of how cultural competency and cultural equity are addressed,
4. analysis of meaningful curriculum, and
5. reflection on collaboration between service providers and classroom staff.

During their time in the field, preservice teachers observe teachers using checklists, short quizzes, and anecdotal notes in formative and summative assessment. Teachers then use this information to develop targeted strategies such as graphic organizers, verbal and physical prompts, rehearsal strategies, and mnemonic devices. These strategies serve as a model of the assessment-planning-implementation cycle for preservice teachers. Preservice teachers also see how materials and lessons are adapted for children with exceptionalities.

During class discussions, preservice teachers are prompted to discuss culturally relevant and meaningful pedagogy. Preservice teachers note languages spoken, materials that represent the cultural backgrounds and values of the children, and ways in which the classroom teachers value children's heritage. Preservice teachers are encouraged to think about culture as more than ethnicity and language, to understand the values that are shared by cultural groups. Cultural equity is promoted as preservice teachers learn that differing belief systems all have value.

As service providers interact with children in the classroom, preservice teachers learn about collaboration. There is reflection on why some children receive services in the classroom, and others participate in a pull-out model. Thus, the fieldwork provides the preservice teachers with rich information about impactful practices with exceptional children.

The course also consists of four hours per week of classroom instruction on campus. Classroom instruction includes mini-lessons, video case studies, small group projects, and discussion relating classroom concepts and theory to what preservice teachers observe at their field sites. Topics cover the history of special education with an emphasis on pertinent legislation, assessment, culturally responsive practice, and an overview of many exceptionalities (autism, neurodiversity, communication disorders, learning disabilities, social-emotional behavioral disorders, perceptual and physical impairments, and gifted and talented education). Early intervention and risk factors are also addressed.

Preservice teachers complete several assignments that enable them to become more competent in supporting exceptional children. They complete written responses to readings, a case study of an exceptional child, a brochure describing their site, and in small groups, preservice teachers present an "activity plan" simulation to the class. The term "activity plan" is used instead of lesson plan as the former reflects hands-on, active engagement of children.

ACTIVITY PLAN SIMULATIONS

While all of the assignments are impactful, this chapter will describe the activity plan simulation that preservice teachers share with their classmates. This assignment is impactful because it encourages preservice teachers to use what they have learned about exceptional children to create activities that are engaging, culturally responsive, and that address the specific needs of individual children with exceptionalities. Preservice teachers focus on one particular exceptionality to gain in-depth knowledge and also have the opportunity to learn from each other as they view the activity plan simulations. Preservice teachers gain targeted skills and strategies that draw on strengths and support development for exceptional children. The assignment can be seen in textbox 1.1.

TEXTBOX 1.1. GROUP PROJECT: ACTIVITY PLAN SIMULATION

Students will work in groups of two or three to present a **meaningful** activity/experience plan that can be used with children who have specific exceptionalities. This would be a plan that could be used in a classroom or childcare center. It could involve a small group or the whole class. In the activity/experience plan, be sure to include some of the dimensions from the CLASS Tool, especially Concept Development and Language Modeling. The plan needs to be strengths-based, culturally responsive, and address specific needs of children with the specified exceptionality. See syllabus for due dates. Specific exceptionalities are as follows:

1. Special Needs Birth through Three (Heward ch.14, only early intervention section)

2. Preschool Special Education (Heward ch.14, only preschool section)
3. Intellectual Disabilities (Children with Mental Retardation), (Heward ch.4)
4. Children with Learning Disabilities (Heward ch. 5)
5. Emotional and Behavioral Disorders (Heward ch. 6)
6. Children with Autism (Heward ch. 7)
7. Communication Disorders (Heward ch. 8)
8. Children Who are Deaf or Hard of Hearing (Heward ch. 9)
9. Physical Disabilities and Health Impairments (Heward ch. 11 pp. 404–420, 427–445)
10. Attention Deficit Disorder (Heward ch. 11 pp. 420–426)
11. Low-Incidence Disabilities (Heward ch.12)
12. Children Who are Gifted and Talented (Heward ch. 13)

Grading: The presentation is worth 10 points and needs to include the following:

- a brief discussion of the activity/experience plan that is to be used with children who have the specific disability, use the lesson plan template on Blackboard, 2 points;
- a demonstration of the plan, role playing, 4 points;
- engaging presentation with class participation, 2 points;
- question and answer session, 2 points.

The presentation should be 15 to 20 minutes. All students in the group need to be involved in the planning and presentation. **The presentation needs to be engaging and interesting to the class! Do not just read from notes.** The presentation can be modeled after the professor's presentation of children with low vision/blindness. The professor will gladly answer questions and offer assistance with the presentation.

IMPLEMENTATION

From the start of the semester, the professor highlights the assignments that need to be completed. This group project—Activity Plan Simulation—is given much emphasis. Preservice teachers learn that this is a group project requiring them to speak in front of the class. They learn that they will need to use professional-academic language, speak in a voice that can be heard by all, and work as a team.

When preservice teachers ask and answer questions during whole-group activities, the professor comments on the use of professional-academic language. Professional-academic language gets contrasted with everyday vernacular. The professor discusses the role of pragmatics and how language is used in different situations, and for different purposes. Preservice teachers are led in an exploration of how they tailor their language. The prompt for exploration centers on "What do you say to your baby, your significant other, your boss, or a police officer if they seek your attention at 2 a.m.?" This leads to a lively discussion with comments such as "Hey baby, go back to sleep [in a singsong voice] . . . honey shut up [to a significant other] . . . yes boss, it's late but I can help you with that . . . [and] officer, yes sir, officer!"

Once preservice teachers understand code-switching and pragmatics, the professor provides support for the use of professional language. For example, when a preservice teacher said, "The teacher in my classroom uses verbal prompts to get the children to look at her," the professor commented, "That was good use of the strategy of verbal prompts; you used professional language, and the whole class was able to hear you. Thanks!" When preservice teachers used vernacular language, the professor would assist them in reframing the statement. For example, when a preservice teacher said, "The kids [were] acting real crazy and the teacher was mad," the professor said, "Please describe how the children were acting. What were they doing? And please describe what the teacher did. Why do you say she was mad?"

After the preservice teacher responded to the prompts, the professor said, "So the children were talking very loudly, moving around the room quickly, and not listening to the teacher. The teacher spoke in a loud voice and she had an angry look on her face." Supports for the use of professional language also occur during small-group work. As the professor circulates among the groups, the professor listens to the language that preservice teachers are using. The professor highlights professional language and reframes vernacular language.

Throughout the semester, the professor supports the preservice teachers in understanding meaningful activities, culturally responsive practices, and components of the Classroom Assessment Scoring System (CLASS Teachstone, 2014) that promote high-quality instruction. These supports occur as preservice teachers watch videos, engage in readings, and discuss observations from their fieldwork. Professional-academic language, meaningful activities, and components of CLASS are connected to the Activity Plan Simulation throughout the course of the semester so that as preservice teachers prepare their plans, they have a continuous understanding of these elements. Preservice teachers take notes from the field sites, videos, readings, and components of CLASS. They use these notes and comments from the professor as they work on their activity plans.

As they work in class during small-group activities, the professor encourages and supports teamwork. There are guidelines for all group-work activities: Everyone has a chance to speak, members of the group respect each other and each other's ideas, all members of the group are actively engaged, groups may divide up tasks in a manner that works for them, and members of the group may ask the professor for help. During small-group work and planning time for the activity simulation, the professor circulates among the groups offering feedback on the teamwork, using the guidelines as a framework.

The preservice teachers use an Activity Plan Template that was developed using the lesson plan model of EdTPA. The plan has the following components:

1. Overarching theme and name of the specific activity
2. Goals, big questions, content-area focus
3. Knowing the learner, characteristics of children this age, sociocultural context
4. Standards and areas of growth and learning
5. Materials, learning environment, and resources
6. Learning experience, spark/launch/introduction, step-by-step sequence of the activity, multimodal engagement, individualization/differentiation, reflection, and transition to next activity
7. Possible extensions
8. Authentic assessment

Before preservice teachers present an activity plan, the professor provides a model demonstration. For several semesters, the professor presented a model activity plan for children with autism. The preservice teachers used this model to create their own plans. At some point during each semester, one group would present a plan for children who were blind or visually impaired. Because the professor is legally blind (meaning that even with corrected lenses her vision is 20/200 or less), these preservice teachers were hesitant and uncomfortable, frequently looking at the professor and asking, "Is that how it is? Did I get it right?" The professor then realized that it might be best if she presented a model activity for children who are blind and visually impaired in order to alleviate any discomfort that preservice teachers may have felt in presenting a disability that involved their professor.

The professor briefly plans the model activity with two preservice teachers. She reviews the assignment and suggests role-play designations, where one preservice teacher would role-play a blind child and another an assistant teacher. The activity is explained to the preservice teachers so that they will be able to engage with the professor and the class in the activity. The specific activity is titled "Exploring Sounds and Rhythms of Musical Instruments." On the day of the activity, the professor explains to the class that this is a model demonstration and that two of their classmates will help the professor with the activity as the whole class also participates.

Before the demonstration activity plan simulation, preservice teachers are prompted to be prepared to discuss the following: 1) general characteristics of children with the specific exceptionality (children who are blind or visually impaired); 2) strategy use for this specific exceptionality; 3) dimensions of CLASS that they observed; and 4) what made the presentation engaging, meaningful, and culturally responsive. These prompts were presented to students on a handout to promote thoughtful responses to the prompts. The handout included space for comments and questions.

After rearranging the room so that there is space to move, the professor leads the class through the simulation, exploring and matching sounds and rhythms of the instruments. The preservice teacher who is role-playing the assistant teacher spoke Spanish and engaged with some of the class in English and Spanish, demonstrating bilingual methodology. This same preservice teacher and the professor also provide support for the preservice teacher who is role-playing a blind child. Strategies such as verbal cues, auditory description tactile cues, and peer support are demonstrated.

Verbal cues utilized include a description of the location of objects based on a clock framework (the tambourine is on the table at three o'clock). Auditory descriptions include detailed information about the instruments (size, shape, color, materials used in construction), information about the actions of others, and information about the setting of the room. Storage bins for the instruments had small versions of the instruments and pictures of the instruments to provide tactile as well as visual cues. Peers model responses to prompts, offer encouragement, and most importantly provide a sense of community, that all are here together.

In addition to language support, other aspects of culture include instruments and rhythms that are used in various cultures. Cultural values of independence, interdependence, and creativity are prompted and encouraged. The class is engaged through movement, dance, song, and interaction with each other. While they are engaged, they also use the handout described above to reflect and take notes.

After the demonstration, the class shares their responses to the prompts in a whole-group discussion. Then they break up into pairs/smaller groups to begin to think about their own presentations. At this time, the groups choose two areas of exceptionality that they might like to explore and present. As the class works in small groups, the professor quickly circulates among the groups and notes their choice of exceptionality (see textbox 1.1). If another group has already chosen their first choice, the group will use their second choice. Occasionally, both choices have already been taken and another choice is made. There are usually 25 members of the class, and with 12 choices, preservice teachers are able to choose an exceptionality that interests them. One semester, a group presented on sensory processing disorder, so the list given is not a finite list.

The semester proceeds in such a manner that after the demonstration by the professor, the groups have at least two weeks before they need to present. During those two weeks, culturally responsive pedagogy in inclusive education, observation techniques, and writing Individualized Education Program (IEP) goals are topics that are covered. During the last 15 minutes of each of these class sessions, groups have time to plan. The professor circulates among the groups, ensuring that they are planning meaningful, culturally responsive, and engaging activities. They are also encouraged to plan via email, FaceTime, phone, and in person if schedules necessitate.

THE ACTIVITY PLANS

Groups present their simulation on the day their chosen exceptionality is discussed. There have been many thoughtful and engaging presentations. One group that was presenting about early intervention simulated a parent discussion group where classmates were parents holding baby dolls. The presenters led the "parents" through infant stimulation, feeding techniques, story time with babies, and socialization.

Acknowledgment of culturally based child rearing practices was evident. The presenters commented on variations in sleeping—co-sleeping, use of bassinet in the room or an adjacent room, use of regular crib from the start, sleep training, rocking babies to sleep, use of music, and method of total silence. Variations in feeding were also discussed with the understanding that "best fed" is an appropriate acknowledgment rather than "breast is best," bottles are cleaner, babies need solids sooner or no solids until 10 months. Toilet learning, independence/interdependence, modes of carrying, and use of language rounded out some of the values of cultural equity.

Another example was a group that presented on physical disabilities. This group engaged the class in a fishing game that taught compound words. The fishing pole was modified so that it allowed for ease of use by children with physical disabilities. Fish were spread out in a big plastic bin made to look like a pond. There was a word on each fish that could be part of a compound word (i.e., cup-cake, basket-ball, butter-fly, tea-spoon, cow-boy, roller-skate). Each fish had a paperclip on it so that it could be picked up with a magnet.

Classmates role-played children trying to find pairs of words that could be combined. They used magnets that had handles to pick up the pairs of fish. The preservice teachers explained that the usual stick with a string and a magnet on the end of the string did not work for a child that had limited use of his hands.

One of the preservice teachers had modified the activity at her field site so that a child with motor impairments could participate along with his peers.

The group presenting also noted that this activity accommodates children with hand-eye coordination challenges, children who need to move, and children who need multiple repetitions to retain knowledge. This was in a classroom that had several pets, including a fish tank. The children in the class had a lot of exposure to animals. Thus, this activity drew on the culture of the classroom.

A group that presented on preschoolers with disabilities demonstrated an activity that promoted matching, sorting, and classification. The same activity could be individualized based on the child's goals. The group called their activity "What Goes Where?" which shows some of the ways this activity could be used.

The group that modeled the "What Goes Where?" activity used effective questions to prompt language for talking about the objects, eliciting responses of texture, color, function, size, shape, and personal experiences with the objects. This activity provides an opportunity to expand children's vocabulary, and to enhance conversation skills as children interact with each other and adults.

The activity plans included a large variety of activities. One group had math and reading activities for children with learning disabilities. Other groups implemented puppet play for children with communication disorders, sensory activities for children with social-emotional behavioral disorders, and research-based photo essays for children who are gifted and talented.

At times groups struggle with engaging the class, using academic language, or speaking in clear, audible voices. Classmates and the professor provide verbal support, suggestions, questions, and prompts. The professor highlights the atmosphere of a community of practice (Wenger, 1998) so that all can succeed. From the beginning of each semester, preservice teachers are invited to consider how to work together as a community in a spirit of cooperation. The professor verbally asks for ideas that could be used to

Figure 1.1. What Goes Where? Can you make your stars look like my stars? What goes with these? What doesn't belong?

create a framework of engagement for learning. The professor writes the ideas on chart paper and all members of the class work together as a group to refine the ideas into a coherent framework.

During each semester the framework consists of similar concepts, such as 1) commitment to creating space for all voices to be heard, 2) reflection on the NAEYC code of ethics as we consider our work with children, 3) understanding that disagreements with others need to be respectful, and 4) maintaining a space that allows the participation of all members of the class. The framework of engagement is posted on the classroom wall and is referred to throughout the semester during presentations and small-group work.

As with the model activity plan that the professor presented, classmates use the handout to actively reflect on the activity plan and to provide feedback to each group. In general, the preservice teachers present activity plans that are meaningful, engaging, and culturally responsive. The plans offer specific strategies that preservice teachers could use during future internships and in their teaching careers. They work well together, displaying good teamwork. The project is worth 10 points (see Grading at the bottom of textbox 1.1); most groups scored 9 or 10.

LESSONS LEARNED

Preservice teachers need to develop competencies to support many different kinds of learners. This impactful practice enables preservice teachers to develop specific strategies for children with various exceptionalities. Professors need to scaffold the learning of preservice teachers. Modeling, feedback, multiple opportunities for practice, and written reflection assist preservice teachers in learning the skills and dispositions necessary for high-quality teachers. Use of the activity plan template and components of CLASS help preservice teachers to focus on specific aspects of interacting with children.

At the end of a semester, one preservice teacher noted, "Before I took this class, I was afraid of children with special needs, I thought I could not help them. Now after watching so many of the activities and listening to the professor, I have ideas of things I can plan for children with special needs." This particular quote is exemplary of the change that many preservice teachers experienced. Preservice teachers developed skills, strategies, and most importantly changes in attitudes from unease with exceptionality to self-competence in their ability to teach children with a variety of learning needs.

The handouts that preservice teachers use during the activity plan simulations provide a format for organized reflection. Creating a safe, welcoming classroom atmosphere gives preservice teachers the space to make mistakes and to learn from their mistakes. After eight weeks of presentations, one preservice teacher commented, "At first I was tired of filling out the same handout every week. Now I see all of the strategies, stuff from CLASS, and what meaningful is. If I don't teach something right, I can still be a good teacher, I just need to think some more and plan different stuff." This quote is indicative of the process that preservice teachers go through as they use a framework to master their craft and realize that it is a reflective practice.

Small-group work takes the focus off of the professor and lets the professor observe the strengths and needs of the preservice teacher. As preservice teachers plan their presentations, the professor can offer targeted feedback. One area that is particularly challenging for preservice teachers is incorporating culturally responsive pedagogy. Many of the preservice teachers thought of culture in terms of language and ethnicity, thinking that the inclusion of heritage, language, and a few simple artifacts (flags, songs, books) was sufficient.

The professor encouraged preservice teachers to think of culture in terms of the values and beliefs shared by specific groups and how those values and beliefs could be incorporated into activities and infused throughout all educational experiences. It is essential for preservice teachers to realize that culturally responsive pedagogy is much more than the external manifestations of culture, that tapping into the shared beliefs and values of a culture is the way in which children and families feel valued, respected, and connected to the educational system. Culturally responsive pedagogy supports cultural equity, positive identity development, and a sense of belonging, factors that are positively associated with academic success and general well-being (Gonzalez-Mena, 2001).

Role-playing provides preservice teachers with the opportunity to embody concepts such as their teacher voice and characteristics for children based on age ranges. In the last space on the handouts (comments, thoughts, questions), one preservice teacher wrote that "pretending to be the teacher in front of the class made me work to talk loud and use words that sounded like a teacher. I even thought about my face and if it was happy." After one presentation, another preservice teacher said, "it was really hard to act like a three-year-old, I had to keep thinking how three-year-olds talk, hold things, and move their bodies." For these preservice teachers, role-playing enabled them to imagine themselves as teachers and to understand the worldview of children.

Overall, the professor learned that providing specific processes for preservice teachers to reflect on their fieldwork, and the opportunity to plan activities for children with exceptionalities, increases self-efficacy for inclusive, culturally responsive practices. This increased self-efficacy transforms the pedagogy of preservice teachers; they have tools to ensure that all children learn, especially exceptional children. Perhaps what is most noteworthy is that preservice teachers gain a strengths-based perspective that leads to greater equity for all children and classrooms where all children can thrive.

RECOMMENDED RESOURCES

Websites

Classroom Assessment Scoring System, CLASS, Teachstone (2014): https://teachstone.com/class/
Council for Exceptional Children (CEC): https://www.cec.sped.org/
Inclusive Schools Network: https://inclusiveschools.org/category/resources/early-childhood/
National Association of Special Education Teachers: https://www.naset.org/index.php?id=resources4specialed01

Readings

Alfonso, S. (2017). Implementing the project approach in an inclusive classroom: A teacher's first attempt with project-based learning. *Young Children, 72*(1), 57–65.
Bradley, J., & Kibera, P. (2006). Closing the gap: Culture and the promotion of inclusion in childcare. *Young Children, 61*(1), 34–40.
Brillante, P. (2017). *The essentials: Supporting young children with disabilities in the classroom.* Washington, DC: National Association of Education of Young Children.
Dalvi, T., Wendell, B. K., & Johnson, J. (2016). Community-based engineering STEM experiences from a second-grade urban classroom. *Young Children, 71*(5), 8–15.
Nemeth, K., & Erdosi, V. (2012). Enhancing practice with infants and toddlers from diverse language and cultural backgrounds. *Young Children, 67*(4), 49–57.

Videos

Activities with playdough, https://www.youtube.com/watch?v=fsnkxNUBRFY&app=desktop
Cooking, https://www.youtube.com/watch?v=_WWBSXweIiE&app=desktop
Intentional teaching, https://www.bing.com/videos/search?q=intentional+teaching+video&docid=608038647538712823&mid=F9EE6655FD30F6A0B399F9EE6655FD30F6A0B399&view=detail&FORM=VIRE, https://www.bing.com/videos/search?q=intentional+teaching+video&docid=6080468079599932302&mid=7D45EDBF47EA499D658B7D45EDBF47EA499D658B&view=detail&FORM=VIRE
Investigating rocks, https://www.youtube.com/watch?v=CupEMB5NIDo&feature=youtu.be
Investigating containers, https://www.youtube.com/watch?v=AyO1GP-mLHY&t=219s
Literacy, https://m.youtube.com/watch?v=rNA59iXOrcw
Play, autism, caregiver specialist collaboration, https://m.youtube.com/watch?v=Vc50HNnPg0
Head Start Trauma Smart—Trauma-sensitive practice, https://www.youtube.com/watch?v=bXzKVpiSzH8&app=desktop

BIBLIOGRAPHY

Baker-Ericzén, Mary J., Garnand Mueggenborg, Mary, & Shea, Mary M. (2009). Impact of trainings on child care providers' attitudes and perceived competence toward inclusion: What factors are associated with change? *Topics in Early Childhood Special Education, 28*(4), 196–208. doi:10.1177/0271121408323273
Bialka, Christa S. (2015). Deconstructing dispositions: Toward a critical ability theory in teacher education. *Action in Teacher Education, 3*(2), 138–155. doi:10.1080/01626620.2015.1004602
Gonzalez-Mena, Janet. (2001). Cross-cultural infant care and issues of equity and social justice. *Contemporary Issues in Early Childhood, 2*(3), 368–371. doi:10.2304/ciec.2001.2.3.8

Heward, William L. (2013). *Exceptional children: An introduction to special education* (9th ed.). Upper Saddle River, NJ: Pearson.

DEC/NAEYC. (2009). *Early childhood inclusion: A joint position statement of the Division for Early Childhood (DEC) and the National Association for the Education of Young Children (NAEYC)*. Chapel Hill: The University of North Carolina, FPG Child Development Institute. Retrieved from https://npdci.fpg.unc.edu/resources/articles/Early_Childhood_Inclusion

Wenger, Etienne. (1998). *Communities of practice: Learning, meaning, and identity*. Cambridge, UK: Cambridge University Press. doi:10.1017/CBO9780511803932

Chapter Two

Creating Voice

Using Mock Interviews and a Parent Panel to Establish Communicative Skills in Preservice Teachers

Christopher J. Meidl and Debra Hyatt-Burkhart

> *For me, the pseudo-parent-teacher conference gave me a space to experiment and hear my teacher voice out loud. Often in our courses in undergrad, our teacher voice manifests in papers or in group presentations, but it is rare that we are asked to stand alone and sit with our developing identity as teachers. This conference felt like one of the official "steps" of hearing my teacher voice and being able to practice with it.*
>
> —Bella Guzzi

Interacting in a professional manner with parents and families of various cultures and life experiences is a necessity in the contemporary space of early childhood education. Aspiring teachers in teacher preparation programs are often able to get significant time in classrooms and through field experiences to move toward skills in demonstrating abilities related to curriculum, pedagogy, and classroom management. But one aspect of becoming an educator they have continually felt they lacked experience in was working with parents. One student explained, "We talk about building relationships with parents and students, and get the chance to build/work on building relationships with students at field, but rarely are there events where we get more comfortable working with parents."

Students in teacher education programs throughout most of the nation get few opportunities to talk with a parent or two. Rarely, if ever, would they have an experience where the preservice teacher, rather than the cooperating teacher, was able to address an issue or conflict that a parent was upset about in regard to something that happened in the classroom. Establishing a professional rapport and skills as a degreed and licensed professional educator is an area that aspiring teachers, who are typically between 19 to 22 years of age, need opportunities for growth in to develop their own voice communicating with other adults.

Having worked in four different school districts, this author felt it was important to share with aspiring teachers some of the challenging contexts leading to a parent or family member visit. Parents or family members have a focus on their child or children, and that lens guides their advocacy, especially if they feel their child has been treated unfairly. Conflict from classroom interactions between a child and teacher or with peers occurs in various contexts. At times, the issue needing to be addressed has to do with academic performance and other times student behavior. Parent-teacher conferences can be spaces with heightened emotional intensity because parents are in a protective or vulnerable mode. Professional educators have to remain calm and keep an event from becoming confrontational and instead turn it into an interaction that is cooperative and establishes a resolution.

In order to help future teachers develop voice and empowerment, a parent panel and a pseudo-conference are used as a formative, performance-based learning assignment in a junior level course called "Family, Schools, and Community." Therefore, the impactful practice outlined in this chapter presents a learning experience in which the aspiring teachers are able to listen to parents' experiences in schools and with teachers, as well as participate in a simulated conference. This learning experience is described in this chapter in the following format: 1) implementation, 2) outcomes, 3) lessons learned, and 4) recommended resources.

IMPLEMENTATION

As this chapter is intended to help others replicate teaching and learning, it necessitates an explanation of not only the approaches being used but also how they are introduced and taught. Within this section, descriptions of what parent panels and pseudo-conferences are are provided, as well as the steps used to implement them, including the support of colleagues. This particular learning is in the last two to three weeks of class as students will have had most of the semester to understand contexts for interacting with parents and develop a sense of voice. The sequence of learning begins with preparation to interact with parents/family members, then the parent panel, and finally the pseudo-conference.

The parent panel allows students to hear from parents about positive and negative interactions they have had with teachers and schools. It typically consists of three to five participants (i.e., parents, colleagues, and individuals from the community) who come in to answer questions preset by me as the instructor as well as questions from the students. The questions relate to classroom environments, teacher conferences, and communication, as well as interactions related to classroom behavior and assessment. The aspiring teachers are provided with an opportunity to ask parents questions about how they view teachers in various contexts (i.e., teacher conferences, academic or behavioral issues, cultural learning, assessment, communication, etc.).

The pseudo-conference is where a fictitious scenario initiates the need for a conference between a teacher and a parent. Colleagues from the school of education and community members serve as parents to discuss a scenario with the teacher, represented by the aspiring teachers in the course. They are able to work through a challenging event as a means to find their own voice and confidence. The pseudo-conference provides students with an opportunity to practice, with feedback, discussing classroom interactions as professionals.

Both the parent panel and pseudo-conference must be planned for thoroughly. Preparation starts with the profiles being shared with students and a colleague from the school counseling program providing training on how to interact positively with upset parents. Students then have some time to ask me questions the class period before the conference. But one of the things the students need to know is that it is not always possible to be ready for a parent or family member who might come to your classroom.

In Preparation

There is not a lot the aspiring teachers needs to do to prepare for the parent panel, as this learning experience is mostly listening and then asking follow-up questions. (As a side note, students often do better at asking follow-up questions when told that this is an expectation of them as future professional educators.) But the pseudo-conference, as an improvisational performance-based learning experience, requires them to invest in understanding parents and families, classroom issues, and a professional approach to conflict. Two major resources are provided in order to help them prepare: a colleague from school counseling comes to talk to them and a parent-teacher conference practice document helps to prepare them for the day. The preparation guide includes online resources, student profiles, and parent-panel questions.

A Colleague from School Counseling

In preparation for the pseudo-conference, a colleague from the school counseling program meets with the students to offer suggestions regarding how to manage potentially difficult and emotionally charged parental meetings. This colleague provides a framework to help the students make sense of and understand the parents' perspective. The school counseling faculty addresses the need for the aspiring teachers to consider how parents may be feeling that their child is being victimized or singled out, or they may be feeling defensive and blamed for the circumstance at hand. Of greatest importance is the need for future teachers to keep an open mind and an awareness of the parents' general desire to achieve positive results for their children. The primary goal is to provide a lens through which aspiring teachers can view parents with empathy and care, even during contentious or difficult conversations.

The counseling faculty member provides the students with an overview of possible strategies that they may employ during emotionally charged conversations. Body language, such as maintaining an open posture, providing nonverbal encouragement through eye contact, and how one can position the chairs for the meeting are reviewed as tools to decrease conflict and increase effective communication. Further, the students are provided with options of verbal interventions that foster alliance and decrease conflict. Teaching university students to use Rogerian counseling techniques, such as reflection and mirroring, and active listening skills contributes to this discussion.

Students are provided with sample "go-to phrases," such as "I hear that you are upset," "I'm glad that we can work together to achieve the best results for your child," "I can tell that this is important to you," and "Your understanding of your child is so helpful to me in learning how to best approach this situation." These phrases are practiced and role-played to increase students' comprehension and comfort with the approach being discussed. The aspiring teachers are expected to add these specific phrases to their vocabulary and use during the pseudo-conference as a means to have an informed voice.

Online Resources

As a means to have aspiring teachers learn multiple viewpoints about teachers, schools, and approaches to interacting with parents, students are provided with various online resources to help them think critically and specifically about how they might understand working with parents. The parent-teacher conference practice document sent to the students describes resources to help them understand parents' point of view, as well as strategies (i.e., to take notes, address needs, and include the child's strengths, etc.) to increase positive interactions during their pseudo-conference. There are three suggested websites that have different focuses that are important for aspiring teachers to understand: 1) parental views that are negative, 2) fear that teachers have in relation to interacting with parents, and 3) approaches to positive interaction during parent conferences from a teacher's perspective. This order was chosen so that teacher candidates start by recognizing that complaints occur in a spectrum from parental preferences about learning to major challenges related to learning or child welfare. This gets them thinking about multiple issues, but the point is not that they plan for every complaint or issue. More so, we end in a thinking space where they are concentrating on positive interactions.

The first resource, teachercomplaints.com, is an online complaint platform. For better or worse, parents can post complaints about teachers (Mathis, 2019). The instructor explains that the aspiring teachers need not believe what these parents are saying as truths, but should acknowledge that they might be criticized for something that occurred or was perceived to have happened.

One example from the site is the following: "I am a very concerned parent who has done EVERYTHING the teacher has asked of me . . . to character shaming saying all the moms are lazy . . . to telling OUR innocent 5 and 6-year-old children to LIE to their parents every single day." The aspiring teachers are warned that they do not have control of the narrative that might be created about what was said or done in the classroom. Aspiring teachers need to be aware that sometimes an inaccurate depiction is created and that to counter that depiction they must act in a positive manner, demonstrating confidence.

The second resource, edutopia.org/blog/rethinking-difficult-parents-allen-mendler, is a website that discusses common fears teachers have with communicating and interacting with parents. In the article "Rethinking Difficult Parents," Mendler (2019) describes ways to reframe a parent's perspective, whether aggressive or defensive. He provides the six different approaches, such as "view parents as misguided advocates" and "appreciate suggestions and re-establish limits." Partially, Mendler's advice should be used to help teachers understand that they might need to format a way to redirect a negative or potentially conflictual situation into one in which classroom challenges become solution oriented.

The final online resource, teachhub.com, includes an article a teacher wrote about how to effectively create positive interactions with parents. Mathis (2019) describes "5 Common Fears Teachers Have About Talking to Parents," specifically during parent/family-teacher conferences. She illuminates the following worries: 1) "parents will act like they have no idea what we are talking about," 2) "they'll share way too much information," 3) "parents are going to be unbelievably nice . . . and completely unhelpful," 4) "they've come in looking for a fight," and 5) "parents won't come in at all." The utility of this article for aspiring teachers is that they are prepared to overcome any anxiety they might have in regard to working with parents. Having solutions helps teachers process challenges calmly and positively.

The intention of the online resources was to have students rethink views about parents and how to validate and support their concerns. Additional guidance for students included the statement "Taking some notes during a parent conference allows you as a teacher to acknowledge and address a parent's complaint." More so, it was explained that using these resources you should make sure you can do three things: 1) understand and validate what parents are saying (don't be defensive), 2) demonstrate the ability to approach the problem as a professional (look for solutions), and 3) be kind and caring and make sure you end on a positive note using courtesy and manners.

The Parent Panel

The parent panel consists of two to four guest speakers. The parents are often individuals known to the instructor who can speak to challenges or issues they have had with some teachers but have often been greatly impacted by a teacher or two who really connected with their child. These parents typically sit in the front of the group with the aspiring teachers wrapped around them in a u-shape set up. The space is designed to keep the group close together.

Questions are provided to the panelists and the student teachers beforehand. The following are questions designed to elicit responses that are organic, naturally coming from experiences:

- What do you want to see and hear when you go into the classroom where your child has to be for a year? What *don't* you want to see and hear?
- How do teachers create a positive relationship with parents from the beginning of the year to the end? What might *not* help create a positive relationship?
- What are some important ways of communicating with parents, involving both giving and receiving information (openness, boundaries, email, letters, journals, special education needs, behavior, academics)?
- How much time should parent-teacher conferences take? What types of resources do you want to see and discuss during parent-teacher conferences (assessment, student work, behavior, tests/benchmarks, etc.)? What are parent-teacher conference "turn-offs"?
- How does a teacher effectively, but without judgment or pressure, identify and describe what parents can do to help their child? What *shouldn't* a teacher tell a parent or guardian?

The instructor facilitates the discussion in a number of ways. Aspiring teachers are encouraged to ask any of the questions provided if there is a special interest in one over the others. This itself is intended to help these future educators to find a voice and the confidence to use it. Often they are timid in the beginning and so the instructor asks the first questions and lets the panelists respond. When there are struggles with making connections with the questions, the instructor often scaffolds the questions with a follow-up question or provides an experience or his own beliefs, for example, based on his own experiences as a parent. The conversations start out fairly explanatory but become quite organic after the audience and panelists warm up.

Once the panelists start to provide context, beliefs about education, and their experiences, the conversation becomes natural and organic in nature. The aspiring teachers start to ask questions and often admit certain fears or worries they have about parents. The panelists typically respond in kind and sometimes critical (but constructive) ways to the student teachers. The instructor usually lets the conversations flow freely, but must keep the group on task because the future teachers who are not speaking often want to get to other questions and so there is a need to remain diligent to moving through four to five of the questions.

The instructor sometimes also has to challenge the student teachers or the interactions of other teachers who were part of a panelist's experience. The instructor grounds the discussion in positive family interactions, emphasizing an asset view of families and tapping into the funds of knowledge that families bring to the learning experience.

The Pseudo-Parent-Teacher Conference

It is truly in the pseudo-parent-teacher conference that the aspiring teachers hear their voice and recognize how it sounds and how to use it. The context is set up as formative learning and so the future teachers do not have to worry about being assessed with a grade on how well they respond to the parents, but instead get feedback from the parent participant who is acting out a role, which can be an endeavor in itself (this occurs in an improv exchange in which participants pull from past experiences and personal knowledge of education).

The parent participants and the aspiring teachers get a student profile for the parent-teacher conference. These profiles are set up as challenging situations and are not simply a friendly exchange. The intent is to create a heightened emotional state in which the parent participants must do a little acting in regard to being upset, angry, worried, or some other channeled emotion. The aspiring teachers often come in anxious because they do not feel they know enough about the situation or the parent, and as this activity is performance based they are simply anxious about the interaction. It all starts with the student profiles developed from the instructor's experiences in the classroom or those of other colleagues or parents that he knows.

There are nine different student profiles (but new profiles are added each year) that provide a tense situation between the parent/family member and the teacher. Sometimes the situation is teacher initiated and other times it is parent initiated (it is indicated on each profile). The following is one example:

> *Uniqua (first grade) [preservice teacher name 1, 2, 3] Uniqua is a bright little girl who does not always maintain focus in class. She asks all kinds of questions and has some incredible insights that the other children don't always make. Her vocabulary demonstrates she has had many experiences and comes from a home rich in dialogue. However, she doesn't like to write. She talks when she should be listening and sometimes distracts the other children when in whole group (at beginning of the day and after lunch). She comes from a single-parent home, and her mom is a professional who works long hours. Uniqua's behavior is erratic during certain weeks when she seems tired and irritable. All her assignments are done correctly and academically she is doing well. This is a conference asked for by the teacher.*

The intent behind the profile is to provide enough information for student teachers to know the situation but remain vague enough that there is not a clear answer for how to solve the issue or identify the problem. The vagueness is meant to represent what happens in the classroom, where teachers can get caught off guard with a narrative they do not know about. Also, having less context creates more options for student teachers to create a voice. They are also advised that the important thing is "to get an idea of how well you can keep your nerve, stay professional and positive, and determine a way to make the conference productive" while the parent participants provide individual feedback.

The object is to have the parent participants and the aspiring teachers find private space to do the conferences. The students are typically put into groups of three so that the other students can listen while their peer talks. Listening is a great skill for these future educators to learn and this provides another opportunity to hone that skill. It also lets them hear multiple voices and starts to create contexts for tough conversations even if it is a role-play. In the midst of the conference, the conversations become organic and real and so the voice that develops is more pronounced than most aspiring teachers thought it would be.

After all the profiles have been worked through in the small group (over approximately 40 to 50 minutes), the class gathers again and has a whole-group debriefing, in which student teachers talk about what they have learned. It also is the time when the instructor shares a personal scenario, in which he had to tell a parent he could not take his son home with him because he was drunk. Real stories make for real truth. The aspiring teachers are encouraged to really own the situation through recognizing how and when their voice can decrease the stress, anxiety, or pain a parent might bring to them and how to positively work through it.

OUTCOMES

The parent panel and pseudo-conferences created various outcomes. The instructor interestingly found that some of those outcomes were intended by design, but surprisingly the aspiring teachers made connections he had not planned. He continues to find ways to improve through self-study and colleague observation.

As the parent panel and the pseudo-conference are two separate activities, the learning outcomes are different. The panel allows aspiring teachers to listen to and understand a parent's perspective in regard to teaching and learning. The future educators start to see through a parental lens in navigating school curriculum, child behavior, and classroom interactions. There is also an opportunity to grow as professionals, enthusiastically engaging in understanding schools, families, and communities from a critical perspective.

While there is no summative assessment of this assignment in which the aspiring teachers get graded, there is formative feedback provided as part of the discussion. The student teachers also have to complete exit slips, which are online narratives of five to ten sentences about what they have learned or questions they still have about working with parents. The reflection process with someone to dialogue with, even if it is the instructor, provides an outlet to develop voice, even if it is a mental voice.

As the pseudo-conference is performance based, the aspiring teachers get a little more nervous than the parent panel because there is no passive way to approach the learning. The instructor lets them know that the pseudo-conference is not a discussion about how to have a conference, but is about being present in a role-play as though it were real. The self-reflection after the conference produces a number of responses in regard to voice.

One aspiring teacher reflected on how she felt, acknowledging she had more of a voice than she realized because of her prior classes: "I was surprised at how naturally phrases would come to me during the scenarios and I think I did well thinking on the spot." Voice emerged as part of who these future educators had become during their teacher preparation program within the context of the conversations. The instructor realized that from a programmatic perspective the university students were pulling from various courses to participate in this performance. Since the learners bring prior knowledge and skills to the course they are beginning to feel more confident and comfortable in their practice, and this impactful practice allows them to articulate their reasoning and decision making.

Other students discussed the observer role during the conference. One stated, "I liked how we were given the opportunity to observe the other people in our class because they had different scenarios." Observing an interaction allowed them to just think about the scenario without the pressure of responding. They also learned that in the midst of a conversation it is okay to pause and think or reflect as a means to process the situation, especially if the emotional levels have increased.

Voice, listening, and understanding became interwoven through some of the interactions during the conference. Some of the aspiring teachers discussed challenges they had even though they felt prepared. One explained, "Even though I had ideas in my head on how to help the student, it was challenging to talk about it with the parent. . . . I didn't know how to start the conversation and organize my thoughts on the spot."

The conference also established broader frames for understanding interactions and recognizing other people's voices. An aspiring teacher explained, "When a parent gets upset or emotional during a conference and it seems like they are attacking the teacher, they are only trying to protect their kid. It has nothing to do with the teacher." And another aspiring teacher connected to the instructor's story: "I really appreciated your story at the end with the dad picking his son up. I always like the real-life examples, and then explanations or advice on how to handle the situation."

In the end, classrooms are stories and good teachers understand how voice contributes to those stories not only for practical purposes, but also as a means to elevate understanding of position for social self-actualization. Social self-actualization in this case means the aspiring teachers understand privilege, systems of oppressions and disempowerment, and also agency and teachers' roles as social justice advocates in the landscape of understanding marginalized families and communities.

LESSONS LEARNED

This impactful practice has contributed to aspiring teachers' understanding of education through the valuable lens of parents and families. Throughout the evolution of this assignment, multiple lessons have been learned. Some of the lessons underline the value of this style of learning for aspiring teachers who might have a limited amount of experiences in various schools, communities, and cultures. In addition to student learning, lessons learned have also informed how this impactful practice is implemented.

University students in teacher preparation programs often have many opportunities to work with and get to know students and teachers in classrooms, in this case, pre-K through fourth grade classes, but do not get the opportunity to ask parents questions. Most of the aspiring teachers at the instructor's institution are between the ages of 18 to 23. So the complexity of understanding how parents and families see the relationship between home, parental values, and expectations with school only happens very deliberately.

There are few field experiences where this can happen for all the students. Therefore, the future educators who have participated in this learning have typically responded positively to this learning experience, as demonstrated in the following narrative: "I learned that you're not always going to know everything going into meetings with parents and it's important to acknowledge this because you have to be prepared to be hit with information you might've not been ready for." The university students walk out of this class with a lot more confidence in being able to communicate and interact with parents professionally and in a positive manner. They have become aware of how to think clearly and calmly (or at least the need to) when interacting with parents, especially those who are upset about conflict that occurrs at the school.

Over time, various pedagogical improvements have advanced the impact of this practice. The preparation material has been modified to help students understand how to use it. Some online resources have been added while others have been removed due to being out of date. Additional student profiles have been added, often as a product of asking new parents to participate in the activities. For each of the sections of the preparation materials, instructions on how to use the materials have increased or been written with greater detail based off of student recommendations through verbal feedback and online exit slips.

The greatest lesson learned from this assignment is that there is empowerment in voice. This makes the need for finding voice so vital for future educators. Unpacking voice empowers individuals to make decisions even when others might not like those decisions, but it also allows for the development of empathy and caring for other people's voice. Future educators soon learn that educational settings are complex and full of voices, and they must use theirs confidently and with integrity.

TEXTBOX 2.1. SAMPLE STUDENT PROFILES

Look for your name next to the student you will be talking to a parent about. The big thing is to get an idea of how well you can keep your nerve, stay professional and positive, and determine a way to make the conference productive. There will be time at the end of this exercise for parent feedback.

1. Pablo (kindergarten) [Student 3, Student 4]

Pablo is a bilingual child of a migrant worker. He appears to try to listen attentively but always needs you to go over directions again. He rarely turns in his homework. There has been no communication with the family because they have no phone and they don't speak or read

English. Pablo's literacy skills are behind those of his peers (according to the school readiness curriculum the school uses). He can't identify all the alphabetic letters or numbers in English and you don't know if he knows them in Spanish. He switches between speaking English and Spanish all day. Because of the readiness curriculum assessment, he is "in need of improvement" in all areas of the report card the district uses. His Spanish- and English-speaking aunt has come in to talk to the teacher.

2. Tasha (fourth grade) [Student 7, Student 8]

Tasha is a fourth grader who gets by in all her academic subjects with a C average. She always seems alone when there is inquiry time, which allows the students to work on several projects either individually or in groups. Tasha has been teased during lunch and recess for being overweight. This teasing has led to some verbal and physical arguments over the last two weeks with a group of three other girls (Barbie, Evie, and Carly). Two days ago when the girls came in from recess, Tasha ran past you and into the bathroom crying. Although you didn't hear it being said and the other girls have denied saying it, Tasha said they told her to, "Take your big butt to a weight-loss camp." Her mother/father called the next day asking for a meeting. This is a conference asked for by the parent.

3. Dora (third grade) [Student 9, Student 10]

Dora is in a second/third-grade split classroom; she is in third grade. The third-grade work seems too difficult for her, leading her to be frustrated and say things like, "I'm so dumb. I can't get anything right." You've asked the principal if you can use some of the second-grade materials with Dora, but she has said the district doesn't allow that. Dora's guardian wants to talk because Dora comes home crying every night and saying that she wants to quit school and that her teacher doesn't care about her. She said that Dora said, "Ms. [PUT IN YOUR NAME] is only interested in me if I get things right, but I don't understand how to read all those words (vocabulary from the science curriculum)." This is a conference asked for by the family member.

4. Langston (second grade) [Student 11, Student 12]

Langston is a biracial boy who does really well in school but is not very popular among his peers. He loves to please you and spends a lot of time asking you if his work is correct, and most times it is. He seems to need a lot more attention from you than other students, and not because of academics. His uncle wants to talk to you because he has noticed Langston becoming less and less excited about going to school. He says Langston has mentioned how at lunchtime and recess other students say, "You're all mixed up!" as a standard joke. They tend to exclude him from all social activities. His uncle helps out Langston's mom as much as possible because as a single mother she has to work double shifts at least four days a week. This is a conference asked for by the family member.

5. Yusuf and Zeynep (fourth grade) [Student 13, Student 14]

Yusuf and Zeynep are twins whose father/mother is Turkish and mother/father is American born. They are academically strong students in all content areas and behave well. At times they sit together at lunch away from other children, but they also have some peers they interact with during recess and sometimes at lunch. The mother/father called the day before and left a message with the secretary that she/he would be in today to talk to you about an incident that occurred yesterday. A small group of children said, "You're terrorists and you're going to have to leave our country and go back to your own." This episode occurred in the lunchroom.

6. Noah (third grade) [Student 15, Student 16]

Noah has diagnoses of Sensory Processing Disorder, ADHD, and level-one Autism Spectrum Disorder. He is very bright, loving, and funny, but has had many learning challenges in the classroom. His behavioral challenges mostly revolve around a lack of social awareness. He also has an incredibly difficult time sitting still at his desk in class. Noah's parent wants to talk to you because past teachers have "chalked up" Noah's poor test scores to the fact that he never sat still in class and struggled to write, so they assumed he was missing too much in class. This parent wants you to know that her son is teachable and also wants you to help figure out how he can learn and be assessed differently while still in a general-education classroom with no wraparound services.

BIBLIOGRAPHY

Mathis, Meghan. (2019) 5 common fears teachers have about talking to parents. Teacher Hub. Retrieved from www.teachhub.com/5-common-fears-teachers-have-about-communicating-parents

Mendler, Allen. (2019). Rethinking difficult parents. Edutopia. Retrieved from https://www.edutopia.org/blog/rethinking-difficult-parents-allen-mendler

Search Results Elementary School. (n.d.). Teacher Complaints. Retrieved from http://www.teachercomplaints.com/complaints/search_results_elementary+school

Teacher-Parent Conferences. (n.d.). Teacher Vision. Retrieved from https://www.teachervision.com/teacher-parent-conferences Teacher-Parent Conferences

Chapter Three

Making Tacit Cultural Beliefs Visible in Early Childhood Teacher Education

Facilitating Video-Cued Discussions with Teacher Candidates

MinSoo Kim-Bossard

This chapter discusses an in-class activity aimed at raising cultural awareness for teacher candidates who may or may not have cross-cultural experiences. Considering the demographic changes within and outside of early childhood classrooms, teachers are increasingly working with more students who may be deemed culturally "different" from the teacher. For this reason, empathy is an essential factor that will allow teachers to understand children and families who come from different cultural backgrounds than themselves. Empathy also helps facilitate learning and meaningful relationships in early childhood classrooms. As a starting point for embracing empathy in teaching practices, it is essential for teachers to reflect on their own culture and become more aware of the cultural terrain in which they are situated.

Some teachers see themselves as "having no culture" because they have only been a part of mainstream cultural communities, but it is not true that these teachers are cultureless or culture-free (Florio-Ruane, 2001). The impactful practice introduced in this chapter is built on the premise that it is necessary for all teachers to be aware of their cultural positioning in order to make culturally sensitive instructional decisions that promote diversity and inclusion. By becoming more aware of their own cultural positioning, teachers can relate to their students and their students' family members with respect and become equipped to address power dynamics that may exist between various cultural communities within the classroom. Through this relational approach, teachers can build an empathetic classroom community that values what children and their families bring with them to school.

This chapter discusses the impactful practice on the basis that all stakeholders in education, including teachers and students, are cultural beings. For this reason, it is important to recognize that there exists the pressure for teachers to remain "objective," or rid themselves of their own cultural beliefs and practices in the classroom by carrying out "self-culturalectomy" (Florio-Ruane, 2001). In describing how culturalectomy functions in schools, Florio-Ruane (2001) explains how "students' non-school lives and associations are 'checked at the door'" (p. 23). I would argue that this is also the case for teachers, as academic attainment becomes the central goal in schools, and people often regard learning and values promoted in schools "as if they were independent of ethnic, linguistic, or social identity" without much critical reflection (Florio-Ruane, 2001, p. 23).

In other words, both teachers and students are cultural beings, and they relate to each other differently based on their cultural positioning. It is impossible to present oneself as completely devoid of cultural influences in education, as culture directly influences child-rearing practices, social interactions, and the definition of "quality" education. Also, cultural beliefs and practices help interpret and establish the norms, traditions, and values reinforced in various layers of the social strata.

The impactful practice introduced in this chapter uses video cues to encourage teacher candidates to critically consider their own assumptions and familiar points of view in relation to beliefs and practices from different cultural perspectives (Schaffer, White, & Brown, 2016). After providing opportunities to come in contact with unfamiliar routines and values through multimedia sources, teacher candidates are encouraged to grapple with a sense of cultural dissonance through a scaffolded dialogue. This process helps promote a critical reflection of what they may have taken for granted as the normative, culture- and value-free classroom practices. This process aims at teacher candidates developing a deeper understanding of their own cultural positioning in relation to children, family members, and institutions of which they are a part.

WHY IS IT AN IMPACTFUL PRACTICE?

An early childhood classroom is one of the first places where children and parents from immigrant families experience the different cultural norms of the society to which they recently moved (Tobin, Arzubiaga, & Adair, 2013). It is also possible that family members from different cultural backgrounds feel confronted or even patronized by societal and cultural values with which they are not familiar. As the demographic landscape in early childhood classrooms becomes more diverse, it is critical for early childhood educators and teacher educators preparing the next generation of teachers to become aware of beliefs and practices that influence their teaching in both implicit and explicit ways.

Cultural practices often function like air for people or water for fish—until you run out of it or are displaced from it, you may not notice the existence of such a substance or its importance at all. For this reason, this chapter discusses an activity to make "taken-for-granted" cultural values and practices visible, and to help early childhood teacher candidates be aware of cultural power dynamics in their classrooms.

FACILITATING VIDEO-CUED DISCUSSIONS

The in-class activity borrows from the key ideas of video-cued multivocal ethnography, a method devised by Dr. Joseph Tobin to elicit explanations of unquestioned cultural beliefs and practices in his cross-cultural preschool study, which compared typical days in preschools located in China, Japan, and the United States (Tobin, 1989). Video cues are widely used as a part of interview methodology in the field of educational anthropology.

It is difficult to recognize and articulate the cultural beliefs and practices teacher candidates are living and breathing on a daily basis; this activity helps defamiliarize one's own cultural values through an example from a different cultural context and through in-class conversations. In particular, the activity helps raise awareness of the interplay between cultural insider and outsider perspectives of various stakeholders in education. Here is an overview:

- The activity starts with asking teacher candidates to think about how they would respond to a situation that could take place in an early childhood classroom, such as students fighting over a toy.
- Next, teacher candidates watch a short video prompt, such as an excerpt from the DVD companion of the book *Preschool in Three Cultures Revisited*, in which a group of Japanese preschoolers physically fight over a teddy bear, and the teacher intentionally distances herself from the children (Tobin, Hsueh, & Karasawa, 2009).
- Afterward, teacher candidates share their responses, including their emotional reactions and observations.
- This leads to a guided discussion regarding whether it would be appropriate (or not) to implement what they observed in the video in their own classrooms.
- Then teacher candidates learn about the rationale behind the decision the Japanese preschool teacher made—providing the preschoolers an opportu-

nity to resolve their conflict without adult intervention—and take some time to reflect on whether they see any value in what the teacher was trying to do in the video based on the rationale.
- Lastly, teacher candidates consider how students, students' family members, and school administrators would receive such an approach in the contexts in which they would be teaching.

Through this process, the teacher candidates have opportunities to reimagine instructional possibilities in the local context in which they work, as well as think about different expectations the families of their students may have. At the same time, they are discouraged from blindly adopting a practice taken out of context without critical consideration. By carefully reflecting on how the practices they see are situated in cultural contexts, instead of being stand-alone practices that exist in a vacuum, teacher candidates start to see their own practices as also culturally positioned, including how what they do comes from a cultural perspective. Their actions can be seen and interpreted from different cultural points of view.

The activity can be adapted using various prompts to generate discussions. For instance, teacher educators can provide assigned readings, such as Tobin (2005) or Recchia and McDevitt (2018) that illustrate the cultural differences in early childhood education and care settings. (The full references of the readings are listed in the bibliography at the end of this chapter.) These readings can help highlight various domains within early childhood education that can serve as sites for cultural negotiation, resulting in tension, discomfort, and confusion. Some of the possible topics discussed in these readings include the relationship between teachers and family members, the amount of autonomy allowed to young children, teacher-student ratio, and conflict resolution. These examples can also model how grappling with cultural dissonances is not out of the ordinary for teachers.

In addition, teacher educators can also provide case studies for teacher candidates to consider as a way to engage them in a cross-cultural conversation in which different values conflict with each other. For example, "New Jersey School District Eases Pressure on Students, Baring an Ethnic Divide," a *New York Times* article by Kyle Spencer (2015), can be presented to teacher candidates as an example of how different stakeholders in education, including the administrators of a school district and various parent groups, can have differing views on what counts as "quality" education. This article discusses the divide between the school administrators who want to ease pressure on students and immigrant parents who desire to see their children given opportunities to excel in a high-achieving school district.

Since immigration is a key factor that brings an array of cultural borders and boundaries together in local communities, teacher candidates can also consider power dynamics between various groups of people who are positioned differently in society. This real-life scenario can help teacher candidates see how different values and priorities, situated in a particular sociocultural context, can lead to challenging yet essential discussions that have a direct impact on students' lives.

While facilitating this activity, it is important to keep in mind that teacher candidates may perceive practices situated in various cultural contexts through different socioeconomic lenses, priorities, and traditions, and may even see these practices as unsafe, unsanitary, or irresponsible. To avoid merely dismissing cultural variations by stereotyping and essentializing cultural communities, early childhood teacher educators need to emphasize that one example cannot represent an entire cultural group. Also, it is crucial to help teacher candidates understand the complexities of how their own cultural values and experiences function as an interpretive framework for what they see.

This dialogue is not necessarily an easy one to facilitate, as perspectives rooted in cultural beliefs and practices are often associated with personal experiences and values. After watching the video together, beginning with open-ended questions, such as "What stood out to you?" and "What was familiar/unfamiliar?" allows for teacher educators to meet the teacher candidates where they are, rather than pressuring or coercing them to perceive what they saw in a particular way.

Starting the conversation by inquiring about the initial observations teacher candidates made also helps unpack any questions they may have about unfamiliar practices featured in the video, discuss any preliminary reactions they had, and compare and contrast responses with other teacher candidates. Articulating similarities and differences between what they observed in the given prompt and the customary practices in which they are immersed can be a starting point for teacher candidates to critically reflect on familiar beliefs and practices with some perceptual distance.

For instance, here are some common responses to the Japanese preschool fight scene from the DVD companion to *Preschool in Three Cultures Revisited*: 1) teacher candidates see the need for teachers to intervene more actively in classroom conflicts between children; 2) teacher candidates are concerned about being held responsible by parents and administrators for any potential physical injuries that take place in their classroom; and 3) the teacher candidates have seen cooperating teachers in the United States who promote autonomy in children, similarly to the Japanese preschool teacher in the video, even though the way they do this may not look the same.

As teacher candidates compare and contrast what they have seen in the video to what they have learned and experienced, early childhood teacher educators can guide the conversation and ask follow-up questions to make meaningful connections between the familiar and the unfamiliar, beyond what is "right" or "wrong." Specifically, teacher candidates can become more aware of what they are familiar with as the "best practice," the influence of different cultural contexts that make particular beliefs and practices in early childhood classrooms acceptable or not, and the variety of practices that exist within a community.

ENGAGING TEACHER CANDIDATES IN CRITICAL CONVERSATIONS ABOUT CULTURE

The videos used to generate critical conversations about cultural beliefs and practices in early childhood classrooms can help teacher candidates establish a sense of relational positionality as cultural beings. In other words, while the provided prompts can only convey limited information about unfamiliar cultural beliefs, values, and practices from different communities, this activity can help one learn more about one's own cultural perspective in relation to how different cultural perspectives manifest themselves in various settings. By becoming more aware of unfamiliar classroom practices and reflecting on the tension that could occur due to differing values and beliefs, teacher candidates can engage themselves in a process of self-reflection and make visible classroom beliefs and practices they may take for granted, thinking through "why they do what they do."

The video-cued discussion described in this chapter can generate a range of responses from teacher candidates. One of the more noticeable things this author heard and felt throughout the activity was teacher candidates' emotional responses. Whether it was a gasp, a grunt, or a facial expression, teacher candidates responded to the unfamiliar practices reflexively. Based on their training as teachers, personal beliefs, and experiences, they quickly reacted to what made them uncomfortable or what they thought was different from the practices in the cultural contexts of which they are a part.

The teacher candidates established various connections with practices demonstrated in the video prompts situated in different cultural contexts, putting themselves in the shoes of teachers shown in the video prompts. When I conducted this activity, some teacher candidates expressed concerns about what they saw or did not see, such as the Japanese preschool teacher not getting involved in the children's fight over a teddy bear, while others acknowledged the value of what the Japanese preschool teacher was trying to do in the video. These teacher candidates shared that the example from the video resonated with them as they and their cooperating teachers have worked hard to instill a sense of self-sufficiency in students in similar circumstances; such as encouraging students to resolve their own disputes and simultaneously discouraging them from being tattletales and telling on each other throughout the day.

As they pondered on how similar approaches or values would work in their communities and where they are teaching, they articulated their positions relationally to practices situated in particular cultural contexts. Considering cultural beliefs and practices are often unseen by people who are familiar with them, video prompts allow for a healthy distance to emerge between teacher candidates and their taken-for-granted practices by providing alternate possibilities. Through video prompts, teacher candidates can consider concrete and authentic examples of cultural differences, rather than imagined or hypothetical situations.

By reflecting on familiar values and routines in an early childhood classroom compared to unfamiliar practices, teacher candidates can practice articulating possibly unquestioned values and priorities they have adapted over the course of their journey in a teacher education program. For example, teacher candidates may have assumed that teachers should intervene in conflicts between children and not consider the possibility of giving more time and space for children to work things out by themselves.

Teacher candidates can go beyond thinking about practices as "right" or "wrong" in absolute terms, and account for the cultural values that influence interpretations of various practices in educational contexts. As teacher candidates learn that the Japanese preschool teacher's response to the children fighting over a teddy bear (or the lack thereof) was culturally appropriate, they can reflect on how cultural contexts can influence how particular cultural beliefs and practices are perceived.

Being able to see oneself situated within cultural values, beliefs, and practices in relation to other perspectives is a great asset as teachers may find themselves in conflict with other stakeholders in education regarding their visions of what counts as "good," "quality" teaching and learning. By examining the relationships between various cultural perspectives, teachers can see a wide variety of practices that contribute to early childhood education and care, instead of insisting on one ideal type of best practice. This process can help teacher candidates intentionally think through their instructional decision-making process, based on the cultural and relational contexts of the classroom, and establish a rationale for their practice.

It is possible that a teacher candidate might still consider immediate teacher intervention an effective way to respond to student conflict after watching the video prompt and partaking in a guided conversation. The value of this practice is not necessarily making immediate changes in teacher candidates' beliefs or in having them adopt those of the teacher educators, but rather it is in generating room for authentic, reflective, and continuous dialogues on the influence of culture in early childhood classrooms.

LESSONS LEARNED

In the process of implementing this impactful practice, there were several factors that spoke to the importance of raising awareness of one's own cultural positioning. In contemporary society, many teacher candidates experience cross-racial, ethnic, and cultural experiences as technology, media, and transportation make it easier to communicate and travel across local and national boundaries. It can be more comforting to surround oneself with people who hold similar viewpoints to one's own, and it is not always easy to approach and understand those who seem different. Making intentional efforts to learn about those different from oneself requires humility, persistence, and self-awareness.

In today's society where both similarities and differences are readily highlighted, it is crucial for early childhood educators to become aware of cultural beliefs and practices that influence daily experiences in and outside of their classrooms. The cultural awareness and sensitivity promoted by the impactful practice introduced in this chapter are key in fostering a safe environment for children and families with different cultural backgrounds who may not be familiar with the "typical" expectations of an American school system.

At the same time, today's world can feel misleadingly small and well connected. Many people may assume the universality of certain values, language, and traditions, such as the English language, due to the cultural access made available through technological advancements. However, cultural differences still exist in both implicit and explicit ways despite the widespread belief that people from different parts of the world know more about each other than before.

For example, Peter Alfandary (2015), an international lawyer, shares in a TED talk his experience of trying to communicate with a taxi driver in New York City using British English, soon after arriving in the United States from Europe. Even though both people were speaking the "same" language, the ways that they communicated with each other (and how they expected the other person to communicate with them) made the exchange a jarring experience. When Alfandary asked, in a somewhat deferential manner, whether the New York taxi driver could possibly take him to a provided address, the taxi driver was confused whether Alfandary actually wanted to go to the address or not. Even sharing a language or other form of communication, something that people may assume to be straightforward to interpret, can bring about misunderstandings.

Instead of considering this sense of dissonance a problem, the cultural difference can help remind us how dangerous making assumptions about one another can be. The presumption that we already know everything about one another because of a common language, technological advancement, or available information should not keep teacher candidates or teacher educators from reaching out to children and their family members to learn their stories.

Lastly, articulating and conversing about one's own position in relation to others is an important skill for teachers to have. Being able to do so without dismissing others, while showing respect, is the first step in undoing the "othering" gazes that can make children and their family members feel ostracized. This transformative process facilitated by video-cued dialogues offers teacher candidates an opportunity to articulate what they may have simply dismissed as disconcerting or incorrect practice.

The impactful practice in this chapter may not bring about the immediate responses teacher educators hope to see. Nevertheless, the meaningful and respectful engagement with one another is an essential means through which teachers establish alliances between schools and local communities.

Trying to learn from those who hold different views and practices, instead of villainizing them or deeming them as "less than" is a challenging task, as it is easy to gravitate toward familiar beliefs and practices. With the assistance of guiding questions, this activity can scaffold teacher candidates to consider the values of what is different, rather than jumping to stereotypes or conclusions about cultural differences as being "incorrect." Raising sensitivity for understanding "others" involves recognizing power dynamics between various groups of people, based on many factors including, but not limited to, race, ethnicity, nationality, gender, and ability.

The impactful practice discussed in this chapter can serve as an impetus for a critical reflection on how teachers and teacher candidates work with cultural differences in and outside of a classroom context. Further understanding why teachers do what they do, as well as considering the importance of what children and their family members can bring to the classroom, can contribute to understanding and addressing possible tensions teachers may experience with people from different cultural backgrounds. As challenging norms can cause a sense of discomfort, uneasiness, and even opposition, it is essential for teacher candidates to take some time to reflect on the ways in which they are situated in local and broader cultural contexts as a starting point for attending to cultural differences that may manifest in their classroom community.

BIBLIOGRAPHY

Alfandary, Peter. (2015). *Myth of globalization*. TEDxAix, France. Retrieved from https://youtu.be/xUYNB4a8d2U

Druckerman, Pamela, Rousselle, Stefania, Solomon, Ben C., & Laffin, Ben. (2015). Explaining terror to children. *New York Times*. Retrieved from https://www.nytimes.com/video/opinion/100000004042437/explaining-terror-to-children.html?mcubz=0

Florio-Ruane, Susan. (2001). *Teacher education and the cultural imagination: Autobiography, conversation, and narrative*. New York: Routledge.

Recchia, Susan L., & McDevitt, Seung Eun. (2018). Unraveling universalist perspectives on teaching and caring for infants and toddlers: Finding authenticity in diverse funds of knowledge. *Journal of Research in Childhood Education, 32*(1), 14–31. https://doi.org/10.1080/02568543.2017.1387206

Schaffer, Connie L., White, Meg, & Brown, Connie Meredith. (2016). *Questioning assumptions and challenging perceptions: Becoming an effective teacher in urban environments*. New York: Rowman & Littlefield.

Spencer, Kyle. (2015). New Jersey school district eases pressure on students, baring an ethnic divide. *New York Times*. Retrieved from https://www.nytimes.com/2015/12/26/nyregion/reforms-to-ease-students-stress-divide-a-new-jersey-school-district.html

Tobin, Joseph. (2005). Quality in early childhood education: An anthropologist's perspective. *Early Education and Development, 16*(4), 421–434.

Tobin, Joseph. (1989). Visual anthropology and multivocal ethnography: A dialogical approach to Japanese preschool class size. *Dialectical Anthropology, 13*(2), 173–187.

Tobin, Joseph, Arzubiaga, Angela, & Adair, Jennifer Keys. (2013). *Children crossing borders: Immigrant parent and teacher perspectives on preschool for children of immigrants*. New York: Russell Sage Foundation.

Tobin, Joseph, Hsueh, Yeh, & Karasawa, Mayumi. (2009). *Preschool in three cultures revisited: China, Japan, and the United States*. Chicago: University of Chicago Press.

Chapter Four

Toward Belonging

Immigrant Family Stories Reinform Perspectives on Family Partnerships

Rebecca J. Pruitt

Children in the pre-primary and early primary grades are particularly vulnerable to the impact of discrimination, as it is during this period that their sense of self and social identity is mostly formed. Healthy formation of these critical components of development depends, to a great extent, on the sense of belonging children feel in their own classrooms. Early childhood teachers play an undeniable role in how this sense of belonging is nurtured, through practices and dispositions that communicate either appreciation for or devaluation of the cultural and linguistic assets these children and their families bring to their classrooms.

Early childhood teacher educators also play a key role by bringing to light and challenging discriminatory dispositions that exist among preservice teachers in their programs. However, biases regarding language and culture are developed over a lifetime and are built from stereotypes that inform views of students and families, thus creating significant barriers for this work (Warren, 2018; Keys Adair, 2015). The impactful practice described in this chapter is designed to facilitate a meaningful learning experience that reinforms the perspectives of preservice teachers to promote positive outcomes for all young children and their families.

FAMILY IMMIGRATION STORY PROJECT

The Family Immigration Story Project is designed to leverage the power of story to move early childhood education (ECE) student teachers beyond learning "about" families with cultural and linguistic assets different from their own toward learning "from" these families. Student teachers become participant observers, as they take part in intimate family gatherings that reinform preconceived notions and unexamined biases. These newly formed perspectives have the potential to influence how they work with children and families by inspiring them to create welcoming classrooms that nurture a sense of value and belonging for children and their families.

Collaborating Through Shared Power: The Key to Belonging

The teacher education program described in this chapter is uniquely designed to prepare preservice teachers for work with all young children and families through embracing the value of cultural and linguistic diversities and diversities of ability. Assignments embedded throughout the coursework are 1) facilitating "critical reflections of their worldviews and racial, social, and cultural locations" (Souto-Manning & Cheruvu, 2016, p. 650); 2) analyzing curriculum for bias; 3) analyzing contexts related to critical pedagogy concepts; and 4) critiquing traditional parent involvement approaches to develop more strengths-based, collaborative approaches.

A critical component of culturally responsive practice is the relationship between teacher and family. Teachers who form authentic collaborations with families through shared power and roles are far more effective in promoting positive outcomes for students than those who adopt a teacher-centered remedial approach (Amatea, 2013). The process of recognizing and critiquing personal biases is an integral component of the development of a collaborative perspective on family engagement. One way to break down these barriers is for student teachers to participate in experiences that connect them in meaningful ways with diverse families (Keys Adair, 2015).

However, interacting meaningfully with families of young students remains an elusive goal for ECE student teachers. "Child, Family, Culture and Community" is a course that introduces innovative approaches that facilitate authentic collaborative work between teachers and families. True collaboration is built from an appreciation for the "funds of knowledge" brought to classrooms by children and families (Moll, Amanti, Neff, & Gonzalez, 1992), but university classroom experiences fall short of adequately preparing teachers for the complex work of collaborating effectively with diverse families in ways that promote shared power and, ultimately, belonging.

Engaging Preservice Teachers with the Power of Story

> Stories "frame the accounts of our cultural origins and our most cherished beliefs."
>
> —Bruner, 1996, p. 40

In an effort to identify a critical learning experience that would assist in facilitating this process, the author pulled from the work of Sylvia Sánchez of George Mason University to develop the Family Immigration Story Project within the course described above (Thorp & Sánchez, 2013). It is not particularly innovative and indeed quite common to require students to interview a family to complete the requirements for a course focused on the family's role in the life of a young child; however, the Family Immigration Story Project facilitates a more transformational learning experience than the traditional family interview.

The elements that facilitate a more profound impact are the rich cultural background of the families themselves, the required method for gathering their story, the required reflection of the students themselves as story-gatherers, and the presentation to classmates. Together, these components comprise an experience that engages students in a personal, critical, and caring way.

Project Guidelines

To complete this project, students must identify a first-generation immigrant or child of first-generation immigrants whose home language is other than English. With this family, they establish a personal relationship that will enable them to become a participant observer for a period of 12 to 16 weeks. Through interactions in various settings, the students gather details regarding birth stories, immigration stories, courtship stories, and intergenerational stories. They must include descriptions of the cultural context of the family, including their formal and informal community networks, and incorporate details about routines, celebrations, and goals.

The following instructions are provided:

> This is not intended to be an interview, but rather an opportunity to gain insight from the life experiences of a bilingual person who is an immigrant or the child of an immigrant. You may offer to provide them a service, such as childcare; attend a community/cultural event with them; visit with them in a community agency setting or school—be creative. Remember, you are not "diagnosing" them; they are teaching you about their family, their culture, their hopes and dreams for their children, their cultural practices.

In addition, students discuss implications for educational practice, including ideas for how a teacher or school could support family priorities. They reflect on how the experience of gathering another family's story has helped them to learn about how their own story has influenced them. Additional teaching and learning experiences within the course have also been designed to promote further processing of the experience of each student following completion of the project.

One such project is the Family–School Collaboration Plan, in which students create a one-year plan for collaborating with families that is built from the priorities and perspectives of the immigrant family from whom they have learned. The presentation of stories to peers (removing all identifying information) multiplies the benefits by exposing students to additional individual stories, many of which are very personal for the presenter.

Project Implementation

All early childhood teacher candidates complete this project within the required course described above. The original design of the project was built from the assumption that most students completing the assignment would need to look beyond the bounds of their own community of family and friends to identify a family of first-generation immigrants. This scenario does play out for a number of the students, and for them, the process of identifying, reaching out to, and eventually spending quality time with a family that was previously unknown to them is a highly impactful experience.

However, as efforts to diversify the ECE student population have fortunately found some success in recent years, many students are now taking this as an opportunity to go through the story-gathering process with their own family; this is an unexpected twist on the original intent of the assignment. These students may choose to tell their family's story through the eyes of parents, grandparents, aunts, and uncles, with some even drawing from their own firsthand experiences. Some students have told the story of a family member who joined the family through marriage, and others who are immigrants themselves or children of first-generation immigrants will choose to tell the story of a family friend or neighbor rather than their own family's story. However, even when this choice is made, these students are inclined to integrate elements of their own experiences as immigrants at poignant points throughout the retelling of their neighbor's story as a lens for interpretation.

Of the remaining student teachers, about half choose to gather the stories of close friends, significant others, neighbors, coworkers, friends of parents, or employers, and some even choose families of their current students. Out of 68 projects completed over the past few semesters, 49% depicted stories of families who had immigrated from Mexico, and the remaining 51% of stories represented 25 other countries of origin.

Gathering Stories

The process for gathering stories follows a similar pattern for students who are telling their own family's story and those gathering the story of a close friend, significant other, or neighbor. Initial meetings usually involve either meeting at the family home or a restaurant. Once the storytelling gets underway, the family participants decide that this endeavor will be better served over a family meal with additional family members present, and therefore, they invite the student back for dinner on a subsequent date.

This same pattern repeats itself over and over in the student reflections on completing this project. Many of these shared meals are part of a larger family celebration, such as a birthday party, backyard barbeque, or holiday dinner. One recent story was gathered in part during a family going-away party, as a family member was preparing to move back to their country of origin.

Other students have gathered stories after attending church with the participant family, or while dining at a restaurant or school cafeteria, going on neighborhood walks, going fishing, or attending sporting events. Some unique meeting activities included playing board games together, visiting a new grandchild, meeting at the gym, and going grocery shopping together at the participant's ethnic grocery store. Participation in these intimate gatherings arguably opens the door to deeper and more personal interactions that enable students to construct a more authentic view of the family's values and dynamics.

Story-Gathering Reflections

Each student completing the project must reflect on his or her experience as a gatherer/teller of a family's story, including a description of the process. In reviewing projects completed over the years, it is evident that there are repeated themes that are common among all of the "story gatherers," themes common among only those who interviewed someone from within their close circle of friends, and themes common among only those who told their own immediate family's story.

All students completing this project express that the process of learning the stories of their participant families was an eye-opening experience for them. For those gathering stories of their own family members and close friends, expressions of surprise at how much of the story they were unaware of—particularly the difficulties their loved ones had experienced before, during, and after immigrating to the United States—are in almost every description.

This realization has led to meaningful reflections on the project for many students, and even deep introspection for some, particularly those gathering stories from parents and grandparents. Comments such as "I have never heard the full story" and "I did not know even half of her story and the hardships that she had to go through" are very common. Many of the student reflections reveal that these students asked questions to complete this assignment that they had never before asked. This assignment pushes students to a more personal investment in the lives of the important people around them.

Students gathering stories from close friends experience even more surprise, as they find that their relationships with these individuals are not what they had seemed on the surface. They begin the project genuinely unaware of how much the immigration journey and surrounding circumstances have defined this individual they thought they knew well. The new revelations seem to have a profound and positive effect on the level of respect and admiration the student feels for this individual and their family. Reflections also show that this newfound appreciation is being generalized to all immigrant families and not just the participant family.

For those who gather stories from within their circle of family members and friends, a prominent theme in reflections on the project is that of a strengthening bond between the student and one or more of their participants. Many even describe this result as a fundamental change in the quality of the relationship, as they begin to see the individual in a whole new light, recognizing sacrifice and commitment unlike any they have witnessed before.

For those that choose to gather immigration stories from their own family, a common theme is the difficulty they experience related to the process of collecting the story. Their conversations tend to uncover intimate details that haven't previously been shared, which is most difficult for those gathering stories from parents. Heartfelt and authentic descriptions of this experience are shared. One student's description sums up the sentiment of the majority of these reflections: "This experience of gathering information has been quite difficult for me because my father's immigration story is actually something my father and I have never fully discussed."

Those gathering stories from extended family members and close friends share similar sentiments, but their reflections usually reveal less personal struggle related to the process. Explaining the revelation from an interview, one student shared, "It was the first time I really understood what it must have been like for my grandmother coming here. I cannot even fathom how hard it must be to be in a classroom trying to learn when you do not have a full grasp of the language." Another student described, "Learning these things about someone like my family member, who I have known my entire life . . . up until recently I never knew about the difficulties he faced as a child growing up here."

Personal Reflections and Presentations

As students move beyond the process of gathering the stories, reflecting on the story-gathering process, and reflecting on the stories themselves, they are then asked to reflect on the impact this experience as a whole has had on their view of themselves as educators. As part of this final reflective piece, they respond to a prompt about how the experience has impacted their calling as a teacher. When the full project is completed, they are required to present it in class to their peers. These two final elements of the assignment together seem to be the key that deepens the impact of this assignment.

In the beginning weeks of the course titled "Child, Family, Culture and Community," which houses this project, students explore the meaning of culture, and in particular their own cultural identities. Inevitably, white students struggle when asked to describe their own cultures. Many feel lost and disoriented, and look for concrete reference points such as ancestors or distant family members who immigrated to America from European countries. References to these countries of family origin are often included in descriptions of personal culture, regardless of how far removed these cultures are from students' own daily lives.

Drawing from similar past experiences in exploring personal cultural identity, the instructor of the course carefully walks these students through uncomfortable introspection. This is generally facilitated through an interrogation of the concept of "normal" American culture and how this damaging construct marginalizes valuable members of our American communities by influencing teachers to adopt monocultural approaches. These approaches incorporate narrow cultural and linguistic models of teaching and assessment that negatively impact the sense of self and social identity formation—a sense of belonging—for children of color and emergent bilingual and multilingual children (Long, Souto-Manning, & Vasquez, 2016).

These conversations are a precursor to the Family Immigration Story Project described here, and therefore find their way into reflections on the stories that are uncovered. As one student recently reflected, "It was hard to hear about her story without getting emotional and angry, indeed almost embarrassed for the way she was treated by what could be considered 'my culture.'" Reflections such as these have the potential to serve as a catalyst for separating white teachers from the power perspectives that have such potential to prevent children of color from feeling a sense of belonging in their classrooms.

Students work to come to grips with the reality of other people's narratives. This was evidenced in the following responses: "I didn't know that people made fun of others for being Mexican," and "I had assumed that they were all the same so one story would be enough for me to understand them all." These new realizations provide ideas for future practice built upon authentic and personal understanding. The majority of these ideas center on student teachers' desire to get to know their students and families as individuals by learning their stories, rather than relying on preconceived notions built from passed down, stereotypical ideas.

Many of the students who investigate their own family's immigration story discover details previously unknown to them. This can create an unexpected opportunity for them to examine the discrimination that has impacted their family's history over time. A number of them share how they have been prodded by well-meaning family members and friends to de-emphasize their cultural and linguistic identities in an attempt to fit in with mainstream societal norms, an experience many describe as dehumanizing.

In completing this project, these students take a bold step by sharing the intimate details of their own family's story with peers through their presentations. Riswold (2016) proposes that professors "are in a unique position to help students examine—and sometimes to interrupt—[dehumanizing] systems and institutions" (p. 74). On many occasions, when students share these personal immigration stories with peers, the subsequent discussions create a scenario by which stereotypes previously unchecked and even unseen by those peers are broken down and reinformed.

TOWARD BELONGING: BUILDING UP AND BREAKING DOWN

Early childhood teacher educators are faced with a complex task in the quest to prepare preservice teachers for the critical work of welcoming all young children and families with a clear message of belonging through shared power and collaboration. No one assignment or experience can provide these results, but efforts can focus on impactful practices that have the potential to serve the unique needs of all ECE students, who each bring individual perspectives to the classroom.

As teacher education continues to focus efforts on attracting a more diverse teaching workforce, we must never neglect to deepen our understanding of how to best support the progress of all teachers toward inclusive and collaborative practices with diverse families. This may require experiences and assignments that have the potential to meet an array of needs, practices that both build up our culturally and linguistically diverse students by interrupting dehumanizing educational experiences while breaking down the biases that may be holding back their peers through interrupting the voices of dominant narratives.

This form of differentiation approached from a learning community perspective can serve to bring these preservice teachers closer together, toward more meaningful and authentic relationships with one another. The Family Immigration Story Project shows promise in creating a unique opportunity for meaningful connections among students that have not been evident in any other learning experience. Ultimately, these connections have the potential to provide the foundation for progress toward the formation of truly collaborative, asset-based perspectives on building family partnerships our young children so desperately need.

RESOURCES

TEXTBOX 4.1. FAMILY IMMIGRATION STORY PROJECT GUIDELINES

To complete this project, you will richly describe a family/community/culture by becoming an informed participant observer in the context of that family's life. This assignment asks you to identify a person whose home language is other than English and who is either an immigrant or the child of an immigrant. Then establish with their family a plan to learn from them. You will need to show evidence of at least two contacts with the individual/family. This is not intended to be an interview, but rather an opportunity to gain insight from the life experiences of a bilingual person who is an immigrant or the child of an immigrant. You may offer to provide them a service, such as childcare; attend a community/cultural event with them; visit with them in a community agency setting or school—be creative. Remember, you are not "diagnosing" them; they are teaching you about their family, their culture, their hopes and dreams for their children, their cultural practices. Your purpose is to get to know them. No real names are to be used in telling or writing the story. You are encouraged to use artifacts or visuals to help tell the story in class, as part of your final presentation.

Paper Outline (6–7 pages, double-spaced):

a. Describe your process for learning what you learned (1/2–1 page).
b. Describe the family. Tell their story. Consider the importance of birth stories, immigration stories, courtship stories, and intergenerational stories (2–3 pages).
c. Describe the cultural context of the family, including the formal and informal community network and system of supports. Remember the importance of family routines, celebrations, and goals (1–2 pages).
d. Reflect on yourself as a gatherer/teller of a family story. What was easy? What was hard?
e. How did this project help you better understand another culture? (1–2 pages).
f. Reflect on how this experience has helped you understand your calling as an early childhood professional (1–2 pages).

BIBLIOGRAPHY

Amatea, Ellen. (2013). *Building culturally responsive family-school relationships.* London: Pearson.
Bruner, Jerome. (1996). *The culture of education.* Cambridge, MA: Harvard University Press.
Couse, Leslie, & Recchia, Susan (Eds.). (2016). *Handbook of Early Childhood Teacher Education.* New York: Routledge.
Keys Adair, Jennifer. (2015). *The impact of discrimination on the early schooling experiences of children from immigrant families.* Washington, DC: Migration Policy Institute.
Long, Susi, Souto-Manning, Mariana, & Vasquez, Vivian. (2016). *Courageous leadership in early childhood education: Taking a stand for social justice.* Teachers College Press.
Moll, Luis C., Amanti, Cathy, Neff, Deborah, & Gonzalez Norma. (1992). Funds of knowledge for teaching: Using a qualitative approach to connect homes and classrooms. *Theory Into Practice, 31*(2), 132–141.
Riswold, Caryn. (2016). Vocational discernment: A pedagogy of humanization. In David Cunningham (ed.), *At this time and in this place: Vocation and higher education,* 72–96. New York: Oxford University Press.
Souto-Manning, Mariana, & Cheruvu, Ranita. (2016). Challenging and appropriating discourses of power: Listening to and learning from early career early childhood teachers of color approaches, strategies, and tools. *Equity and Excellence in Education, 49*(1), 9–26.
Warren, Chezare A. (2018). Empathy, teacher dispositions, and preparation for culturally responsive pedagogy. *Journal of Teacher Education, 69*(92), 169–183.

Chapter Five

Listening to Voices of Families as a Transformative Process

Julia Ann Williams

Transformative experiences are integral to the development of early childhood teachers in a global society. Gonzalez-Mena (2008) defines transformative education as "an experience when two people or groups come together and interact in such a way that both are transformed . . . it comes from respectful interactions and ongoing dialogue" (p. 25). An essential part of transforming future educators is getting them to recognize the various people involved in the learning process. It is essential to get them to consider the power in community building as it relates to teachers, parents, and children. Quijada Cerecer (2011) discusses the importance of relational engagement, in which students seek a sense of community; teachers and children desire to have connections with each other.

Connectedness or relational engagement not only can be an effect but also can be a cognitive experience where space can be provided for intellectual growth and insights about any topic or issue. Each member in such a space can benefit and learn to value the lived experiences of others and create a sense of community. This concept can be transferred to working with families. As most teacher educators believe relational engagement is important, it is crucial they can model for preservice teachers how to create such an environment in which parents, students, and teachers experience a sense of community. The concept of relational engagement is participatory and active. It is grounded in the premise that each member appreciates, respects, and listens to the differences in worldview that ultimately inform and improve practice.

There is a need to restructure teacher education preparation programs so that preservice teachers are more prepared to teach a diverse population of students (Ball, 2009; Gay, 2010; Gonzalez-Mena, 2008; Kinloch, 2011). Part of this process involves providing experiences for preservice teachers to self-reflect on their attitudes and preconceived notions about the different socioeconomic and cultural backgrounds of children, and to recognize personal biases. Two challenges arise for instructors trying to transform teacher educators: candidates have limited experiences 1) working with diverse populations, and 2) being taught by a professor of color.

This teacher educator is recommending a "multivoiced approach" that listens to the voices of parents across different socioeconomic and cultural backgrounds to gain insights about what they truly want and need in partnering with early childhood teachers in their child's education. Kinloch (2011) called it "democratizing engagement" as it relates to children. A multivoiced approach includes the preservice teacher, the teacher educator, and the family working with and listening to each other. Learning to value multiple voices in teacher preparation allows preservice teachers to develop this skill as part of their teacher identity and ultimately improve the educational experiences of young children.

IMPACTFUL PRACTICE

The underlying challenge is to be able to recognize the historically researched and documented issues that have permeated the U.S. educational system, including higher education and preservice teachers' and teacher educators' understanding of coevalness (O'Garro & Duncan, 2007). Coevalness indicates that teachers, preservice teachers, and parents coexist together. The desire to inform and create a community of learners requires coevalness. Teacher candidates need to recognize the importance of valuing the lived experiences of the teacher educator, as a woman of color, as she teaches them how to create relationships with parents. Preservice teachers are provided with deliberate and valuable experiences in two courses that will be shared later in this chapter.

The expertise of the teacher educator is designed to help the teacher candidates be prepared for teaching methods and strategies meant to help them build relationships with parents in two courses. If the teacher candidates consider the teaching methods and content too different from their past experiences or not equal to what they view as valuable, this could cause "dysrhythmic conditions" (Duncan, 2005).

A dysrhythmic condition is an environment where the participants—in this case preservice teachers and the teacher educator—are not in sync with each other as it relates to the relevancy of the topic or curriculum. For example, if the teacher educator is teaching about a topic that applies to an age level the teacher candidate is not interested in, then the candidate will dismiss the relevance and importance of the subject and devalue the knowledge of the teacher educator based on their disinterest.

With the goal of producing a community of learners, the classroom environment and activities must include developing particular attributes such as compassion, nurturance, and love in the teacher candidates. When these traits are produced as part of the "teaching" context of the university classroom, teacher candidates not only develop the traits but also learn how to emulate these qualities in other environments, especially when working with children and families. Therefore, these learning goals are implemented in two courses.

Within the courses "Integrated Curriculum" and "Family, School, and Community," there are specific assignments and class activities that aim to be transformative in nature. Transformation—incorporating the development of compassion, nurturance, and love—is targeted explicitly around preservice teachers' ability to understand diverse populations. They learn to respectfully receive cultural variation in their classroom and build skills for working collaboratively alongside the parents/families of young children.

In the Integrated Curriculum course, the focus age group is children in preschool and kindergarten. Preservice teachers are expected to use their prior knowledge of child development to consider and plan developmentally appropriate experiences for this age group. However, before planning the activity the teacher educator provides a foundational context focusing on positionality that preservice teachers need to keep in mind when planning and implementing curriculum.

For example, significant factors about the population of the children need to be considered, such as social and cultural context, social and economic status, prior early learning experiences, educational resources available, and home and community environments. In order to engage the preservice teachers in considering these factors, multiple transformative experiences are introduced. Several weeks are spent engaging the preservice teachers in discussions about diverse populations through various media (e.g., case studies, antibias curriculum books, videos) depicting how teachers consider diversity in their classrooms, with experts from different classrooms demonstrating how they include diverse experiences for young children.

After viewing the example classrooms, in-class follow-up discussions are facilitated by the teacher educator so the preservice teachers reflect on discourses about diverse students, families, and communities. The strength of the impactful practice is that it is completed in a learning environment that allows students freedom to express themselves and listen to the thoughts and feelings of others related to privilege, oppression, social injustice, multicultural perspectives, and so forth. These experiences are scaffolded to allow for a deeper immersion into each topic.

Preservice teachers are at times unaware of how their privileges in their early development have impacted their worldview. They are sometimes unaware of how their worldview could impact how they perceive and respond to others that are unlike them. This can be a challenge to address, especially for a teacher educator of color. The scaffolding as it applies here is being able to begin the conversation where the students are, which means allowing them to discuss what they can recall about their own early learning experiences and other topics such as the racial and economic implications of locations in which they have chosen to engage with young children.

This discussion includes all of the factors that should be considered when planning for young children. The teacher educator asks the preservice teachers the following questions: What type of early experiences were you engaged in? What do you recall learning in those experiences? What extracurricular experiences did you have? What resources were available in your home? How diverse were the children in your early experiences? What community experiences were you able to engage in (such as going to the zoo, aquarium, summer vacations, field trips, etc.)?

After the preservice teachers share their experiences, the teacher educator then injects the "what ifs" to change the narratives; for example, what if the children came from limited home resources? What if the early program experiences were under-resourced and lacked quality educational experiences and positive engagements? What if the children lacked security and safety in their community environment? What if the teachers that were engaged with the children had low expectations of what they were able to accomplish? What if most of the children never experienced vacations, field trips, the local zoo, and other educational resources available in the community?

From this teacher educator's experience, having the preservice teachers reflect on their own narrative first reduces the tension they may feel about living in privileged conditions and having limited diverse experiences. Allowing them to share their worldviews helps them recognize the importance of listening to the worldview of the teacher educator, as a woman of color, and the perspectives of families and communities different from their own.

Two courses taken, one during their sophomore year and the other their junior year, engage the preservice teachers in intentional exercises to prepare them to work with diverse families. The first course that will be discussed is the Integrated Curriculum course, which is offered in the spring of the preservice teachers' sophomore year. Its focus is on curriculum design and implementation for children attending preschool and kindergarten. The second course is the Family, School, and Community course, which focuses on considering the many factors that can have an impact on children and families as well as supports that can be provided through community resources. Prior to these two courses, the preservice teachers have separate courses focused on social justice in educational settings. The two courses utilize various experiences that the preservice teachers participate in as a means to strengthen their knowledge, skills, and dispositions when working with children and families.

The first experience for the preservice teachers is in the Integrated Curriculum course. As stated earlier, this course is designed to review the various philosophies that early childhood programs may embrace and discusses multiple factors to be considered when planning a program and curriculum. The two foundational tenets for this course are developmentally appropriate practice, established by NAEYC (2009), and antibias curriculum, based on writing by Derman-Sparks, LeeKeenan, and Nimmo (2014). Developmentally appropriate practice (DAP) informs the preservice and in-service teachers about practices for pedagogy and curriculum that are age appropriate, individually appropriate, and culturally appropriate. Antibias curriculum provides the context for addressing how to strengthen the individual child's identity as well as identify and challenge bias and inequities in the lives of young children, their families, and the community at large; this approach emphasizes empathy toward others and develops an understanding of multiple perspectives. For early childhood teachers, these two tenets need to be the driving force for creating and establishing any program that effectively engages children and families.

In order for preservice teachers to understand DAP and antibias curriculum, they have to see examples of how these occur in the learning of young children, whether they are adapting established curriculum or scaffolding children's learning. Often, candidates rely on curriculum activities found on the Internet and neglect to evaluate the developmental appropriateness and effectiveness of the activities. For example, a preservice teacher may identify an activity for families to complete at home that seems fun and engaging but requires not readily available or costly materials. Another example would be a preservice teacher neglecting to consider if a child would be able to successfully complete an activity based on the developmental age of the child and what specific skills they would learn by engaging in the activity, such as emphasizing writing when the child is not ready.

Systematic instruction is needed to help preservice teachers evaluate how and why the chosen activities could be effective for young children, but always in the context of the socioeconomic and cultural backgrounds of the participants. The preservice teachers are taught to consider instruction by using the lens of the population they will be engaging. Several class sessions are designed for the instructor to model for them how to implement opening songs and finger plays with young children, which is followed by small-group peer practice. These in-class sessions allow for a safe environment for them to receive constructive feedback from the instructor and their peers for improving their teaching and learning practices.

During these reflective sessions, it is important to refer back to the early learning standards and the developmentally appropriate practices to determine if the suggested activities and curriculum planning meet the criteria. Oftentimes, the teacher educator only facilitates the discussion and encourages the peers of the preservice teacher to provide constructive feedback. The teacher educator asks the preservice teacher to identify elements of the activity or curriculum that meet the criteria of being antibias and developmentally appropriate.

In the Family, School, and Community course, several assignments work together to help preservice teachers understand the complex nature of working with diverse children and families. This course is divided into three components: families and schools in urban settings, discourse with community guest speakers, and a "community of learners" project. The first component provides instructional background about families and schools in urban settings. The preservice teachers research key educational theorists and their philosophies as they relate to culturally relevant pedagogy and environments. A few of the key focus areas highlighted during instruction are 1) assumptions about parent involvement, 2) parent–school partnerships, 3) parents as advocates, 4) creating a culture of involvement, and 5) the ecological systems theory.

The next portion of the course consists of the community guest speakers, who come and share their wisdom and expertise with the preservice teachers. The topics addressed include homelessness, addiction, incarcerated parents, trauma, bullying, fatherhood, family engagement, school administration, and inclusive spaces in schools. After each presentation, there is a question and answer period with the community guest. During the next class period, deeper reflection as a class occurs when small groups gather and discuss the critical portions of the presentations that had meaning to them as developing teachers.

Since the course is designed to address urban education and working with diverse populations, the discourse or dialogue between the preservice teachers, faculty instructor, and guest speaker can be very transforming. Such transformation is reminiscent of the work by Ball (2009). Using her zone of generativity model, she addresses how preservice teachers and teacher educators impact each other in a bidirectional interaction of informing and discussing educational issues with each other.

Although such discussions can be uncomfortable for some individuals, they often lead to positive change not only for the preservice teacher but also for the teacher educator. If this model is extended to include parents, educators will have an improved understanding of others' perspectives and how parents and teachers can work together more effectively to the benefit of children.

The final component of the course assignment is for preservice teachers to experience a "community of learners" project. The undergraduate preservice teachers collaborate with the graduate preservice teachers to plan and implement a community-based, Saturday morning, literacy experience for preschool children and their parents. These sessions provide an opportunity for the preservice teachers to have first-hand engagements with children and parents.

This component is called the "community of learners" because it is intentionally linked with the graduate preservice teachers to implement the sessions. This was an intentional endeavor so that all of the preservice teachers could realize that regardless of their level of study in the program they can effectively collaborate to have a positive impact on children and families. The graduate preservice teachers enrolled in the early literacy course work in small groups to plan and implement learning stations centered on a specific book each week; they also plan and implement a mini-workshop for parents each week. The undergraduate preservice teachers are responsible for identifying supplemental materials to support the parent workshop theme each week and providing a snack for the children. All supplemental materials are compiled in a family friendly packet that includes extended activities that can be done at home based on the book for the week.

IMPLEMENTATION

In the Integrated Curriculum course, the teacher educator becomes the facilitator of learning and serves as the model for implementing instruction. Several sessions are designed to provide engaging hands-on activities for the preservice candidates to see how to plan and implement opening activities. The teacher educator brings in several resources such as audio CDs of music representing diverse cultures, children's literature with antibias themes, finger play activities, and rhymes and songs that can be implemented with young children.

Modeling how stories and songs should be introduced and shared with young children provides a concrete example of how to incorporate cultural competence. For example, one story that was shared with the class was *Aunt Flossie's Hats*, by Elizabeth Fitzgerald Howard. This is a culturally relevant story that depicts the impact of oral storytelling and literacy. To provide a setting for the preservice teachers to observe, the teacher educator softly played African instrumental music and brought in several hat boxes. One hat box was opened, and a fancy green decorative hat was shown to the class. The class discussed where children would see such a hat.

Since this was a story about an African American family, some suggested that the hat could be worn at special events or church. The teacher educator, who is African American, shared her love for hats and discussed the various hats she has worn. Stories are read to the class with a follow-up discussion, including possible extended activities that could be implemented based on the content of the story (Gay, 2010).

After weeks of modeling and practice, the sequence moves to giving the teacher candidates responsibility for dividing into groups to plan opening activities that include a story, songs, and finger plays. Students are able to implement the previously modeled format in the university classroom to preschool-age children from a local childcare center. This provides another opportunity for the preservice teachers and the teacher educator to reflect on the practices modeled by the teacher educator and what was implemented by the preservice teachers; this leads to a discussion about what went well in the presentations and what should be changed for next time.

Since this model of reflection is general in practice, the reflecting and sharing time occurs with an attitude of respect and professional growth. Preservice teachers also evaluate the effectiveness of the presentation and share suggestions as to what they would have included in the teacher educator's presentation to enhance the experience. This back-and-forth dialogue between the preservice teachers and the teacher educator is designed to be transformative and generative.

In the Family, School, and Community course, following weeks of in-class discussion about culturally relevant practices and environments in a variety of communities, guest speakers come and share their expertise on a variety of topics. Speakers are invited to provide a narrative on the following topics: father engagement in schools, inclusive and exclusive places in schools, parent and child advocacy, what superintendents look for when hiring teachers, the impact of addiction on the child and family, homelessness and school support, and bullying. Following each presentation, a debriefing/reflection session allows students to process and discuss the information shared.

This open dialogue is so critical to the overall professional development of the preservice teacher and the teacher educator. The conversations between the small groups of students occur using the "fishbowl" technique, beginning with quiet, short comments. As the other class members listen they take the place of a classmate in the "fishbowl" to continue the conversation. As the conversation continues the discussions and reflections offer deeper and deeper context and criticalness. Each class member becomes engaged in the conversation, and all offer their opinions in an environment that they feel is safe enough to share openly in. These are precious moments in a classroom, when preservice teachers and the teacher educator can truly have an authentic discussion revealing the inner thoughts of each person, where participants are a "community of learners."

One final goal of the course assignments is for the students to experience a "community of learners" project. The undergraduate preservice teachers from the course collaborate with graduate preservice teachers to plan and implement a community-based, Saturday morning, literacy experience for preschool children and parents. The responsibility of the undergraduate preservice teachers is to create an extension activity packet for the families to implement at home focusing on the selected book of the week. Each group of four to five preservice teachers plan for one of the four Saturday sessions; the plan includes extension activities and the groups provide a snack for their assigned session. This experience also allows them to work with graduate preservice teachers and to see the coordination of all students toward the same goal: to provide engaging experiences for families.

One example of this "community of learners" project included the story *I Like Myself!* by Karen Beaumont. The graduate preservice teachers decided to focus on self-care strategies with the parents, while children explored activities to support what they like about themselves. Activities for the children included a body puzzle, an "I like myself" worksheet with picture stickers they put on body shaped paper, and the song "Head, Shoulders, Knees, and Toes." The topic for the parents was "What does self-care mean to me?" The preservice teachers planned an ice-breaker exercise for them to talk about what they currently do for self-care. The group followed up with creating a self-care booklet and making a play-doh stress ball. The undergraduate preservice teachers disseminated a handout that included "how to teach our child self-care strategies," 50 positive thoughts and affirmations for children, a self-care independence checklist, and a handout on how to help children develop their own self-care plan. The undergraduate preservice teachers also provided a snack that consisted of carrots and apples, which supports healthy eating.

LESSONS LEARNED

The opening activities assignment has been quite successful. Many of the preservice teachers mentioned that it was very different actually implementing the opening activities. What they had envisioned for the most part did not happen. They did not expect comments from the children about parts of the story. For example, one group read, *The Day the Crayons Quit* by Drew Daywalt. In the story, one crayon took off his paper wrapping and was "naked." The children were so focused on the "naked" concept that they laughed and laughed, and it was a challenge to bring the children back to the story so that the reader could finish reading.

Another example was when the preservice teachers planned a finger play that had too many parts. The teacher educator explained that if the preservice teachers selected a finger play with several parts, they should provide some props that would help the children remember the different parts of the finger play. This particular group selected a finger play with too many parts to remember and no props, and the children had difficulty following along and became disengaged. The preservice teachers learned that props can be very useful in teaching a new finger play.

The preservice teachers experience firsthand that lessons do not always go as planned or expected. When they practice presenting to each other everything goes fairly smoothly. However, with children challenges arise; the planned story, songs, and finger plays may take longer to implement; the children ask questions and may make comments not related to the activities; and preservice teachers have to learn how to get the children back on track. The challenge of effectively engaging the children led to an authentic learning experience.

The community engagement project is still a work in progress. Some areas that need to improve are the intentional connections and collaborations with the graduate preservice teachers and identifying common times for students to meet and physically work together. Another area for improvement is getting increased interest from preservice teachers about coming in on the select Saturdays. This would allow them to observe the family workshops, as well as assist the children participating in activities. An option that could be considered is for the preservice teachers to select how they would like to be involved in the Saturday sessions through an activity contract. They could select from a listing of involvement that would include attending the sessions, providing the snacks and newsletters, or assisting with the promotion of the event by creating and disseminating fliers to participating centers.

Overall, the Saturday sessions have been engaging, leading families to return and new families to join. The experience has led to undergraduate and graduate preservice teachers working together collaboratively. It has reduced some of the anxiety some students have about presenting to parents and working with young children. It has also taught undergraduate and graduate preservice teachers how to collaborate and plan events effectively as a team. For the teacher educator, it has required considerable attention to detail about how to model instruction, provided opportunities for practice, and improved the debriefing and reflection process after each session.

IN CONCLUSION

Getting preservice teachers to understand that people in communities are all connected and impacted by each other is at the center of this impactful practice. Each time individuals come together, change occurs through the experience of verbal and nonverbal interactions. This change has the potential to transform one's thinking, mindset, and attitudes about self and others; and allows preservice teachers to see themselves as leaders and use their agency to contribute to the school and neighborhood community. Teacher educators must be inclusive and embrace their students, families, and the communities they serve. Hopefully, when the preservice teachers think about communities and families, they say to themselves, "I am a part of this community (their own classroom, school, colleagues, etc.), and I want this community to help me make a positive impact on families that will ultimately also change me!"

BIBLIOGRAPHY

Ball, Arnetha F. (2012). To know is not enough: Knowledge, power, and the zone of generativity. *Educational Researcher*, *41*(8), 283–293.

Ball, Arnetha F. (2009). Toward a theory of generative change in culturally and linguistically complex classrooms. *American Educational Research Journal*, *46*(1), 45–72.

Derman-Sparks, Louise, LeeKeenan, Debbie, & Nimmo, John. (2014). *Leading anti-bias early childhood programs: A guide for change*. New York: Teachers College Press.

Duncan, Garrett Albert. (2005). Critical race ethnography in education: Narrative, inequality and the problem of epistemology. *Race Ethnicity and Education*, *8*(1), 93–114.

Gay, Geneva. (2010). *Culturally responsive teaching: Theory, research, and practice*. New York: Teachers College Press.

Gonzalez-Mena, Janet. (2008). *Diversity in early care and education: Honoring differences*. Boston: McGraw-Hill.

Kinloch, Valerie. (2011). Crossing boundaries studying diversity: Lessons from preservice teachers and urban youth. In A. F. Ball & C. A. Tyson (eds.), *Studying diversity in teacher education*. Lanham, MD: Rowman & Littlefield, 153–170.

NAEYC. (2009). Developmentally appropriate practice in early childhood programs serving children from birth through age 8. Retrieved from https://www.naeyc.org/sites/default/files/globally-shared/downloads/PDFs/resources/position-statements/PSDAP.pdf

O'Garro, Joseph Glynis, & Duncan, Garrett Albert. (2007). Chapter ten: Language, literacy, and love: The denial and restoration of coevalness at an urban elementary school. *Counterpoints*, *310*, 199–218.

Quijada, Patricia D. (2011). Power in community building: Learning from indigenous youth how to strengthen adult-youth relationships in a school setting. In A. F. Ball & C. A. Tyson (eds.), *Studying diversity in teacher education*. Lanham, MD: Rowman & Littlefield, 171–182.

Chapter Six

A Pattern of Practice

The Fabric of a Playful, Active Learning Community

Laurel L. Byrne

Please accept this invitation to join one early childhood teacher educator on a journey of exploration and discovery of an approach to course design that illuminates the synergy resulting from a *pattern of practice* for creating a playful, active learning community. Along this journey, the reader will see how the pattern of practice is intentionally threaded throughout early childhood teacher preparation course design such that the pattern of practice helps to fashion a playful, active learning community that fosters positive relationships and rich, meaningful learning experiences. At its essence is an early childhood teacher education course that emphasizes a "practice what you preach" approach to playful learning.

WHAT IS A PATTERN OF PRACTICE?

One definition of a pattern is a form or model proposed for imitation (Merriam Webster, s.v. "pattern"). The pattern of practice presented in this chapter is meant to serve as a model to guide course design. The pattern of practice serves a twofold purpose. First, the pattern of practice serves as a model for early childhood teacher educators to guide the careful construction of course design. Second, the pattern of practice is fashioned to replicate a model for preservice/in-service teachers to employ in their own practice and classrooms. Figure 6.1 illustrates the threading together of the six essential elements of the pattern of practice: 1) an invitation to learning on the first day, 2) engaging with course material, 3) extending the learning community, 4) documenting learning, 5) embracing the joy of the profession on the last day, and 6) engaging in reflective practice.

Threading together each of the six elements throughout course design from the start of the semester through the last day, underscores the impact of the pattern of practice coming together as a whole and creating the fabric for a playful, active learning community. The main topics in this chapter will include implementing a pattern of practice, outcomes linked to the pattern of practice, lessons learned from reflection on the pattern of practice, and enhancing one's pattern of practice. In culmination, resources are recommended to scaffold the readers' creation of their own pattern of practice to foster a playful, active learning community, enhancing professional preparation as meaning-making for preservice and in-service teachers.

Part of what informs this author's pedagogy is Project Zero's "pedagogy of play" and the indicators of playful learning research (follow the link in the Recommended Resources section). Underpinnings of playful participatory research embraced by Project Zero's pedagogy of play promote a culture of inquiry around one's practice and exploration of innovative ideas "with teachers acting as agents of play and playfulness" (Baker et al., 2016, p. 3).

This teacher educator defines playful, active learning as a learner-centered environment that fosters a sense of joy, wonder, belonging, and meaning-making. It is through the implementation of the pattern of practice that the playful, active learning comes to life in teacher preparation coursework,

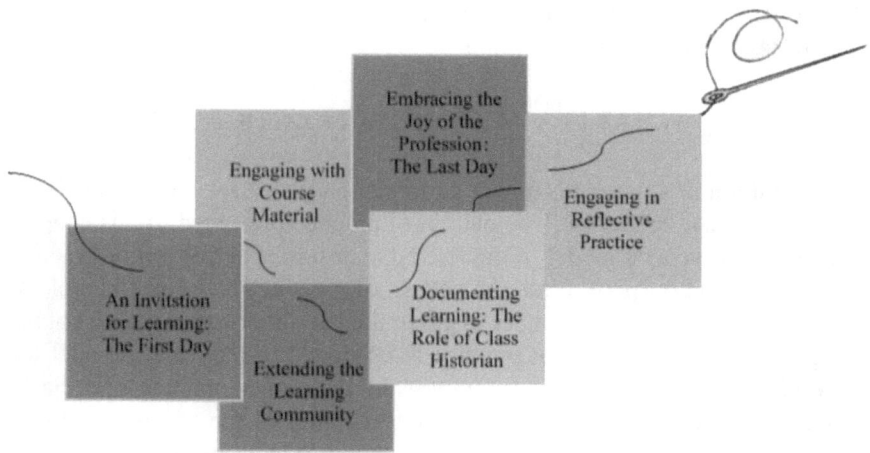

Figure 6.1. Threading together the six essential elements of patterns of practice.

which not only applies a theoretical framework to support practice but also impacts accountability to standards for professional preparation.

The pattern of practice aligns common threads woven throughout course design reflective of the National Association for the Education of Young Children (NAEYC) Standards for Early Childhood Professional Preparation. NAEYC's Standards for Early Childhood Professional Preparation Position Statement states the following:

> Just as children learn best from teachers who use responsive and intentional strategies, adult students learn from instructors who create a caring community of learners, teach to enhance development and learning, plan curriculum aligned with important learning outcomes, assess student growth and development related to those outcomes, and build positive relationships with students and other stakeholders in the program. (National Association for the Education of Young Children, 2009, p. 5)

The pattern of practice described in this chapter illustrates how the intentionality of course design strives to create such a community of learners.

IMPLEMENTING A PATTERN OF PRACTICE: PROMOTING PLAYFUL, ACTIVE LEARNING

Creating a collegial environment that fosters trust and mutual respect and embraces the strengths that learners bring to the learning environment is essential. From the beginning of each semester, it is vital for learners to feel comfortable and develop ownership and a sense of belonging in a learning environment. The six elements of the pattern are described in detail throughout this section, beginning with how the stage is set to emphasize the interplay between essential knowledge, skills, and dispositions necessary for students to understand themselves as both playful learners and playful teachers.

Element 1. An Invitation to Learning: The First Day

An essential element of the pattern of practice is the first day of class. The first day of class is marked by an invitation extended to the students to join the learning community on a joint venture of inquiry, discovery, and exploration related to the course content. The invitation to learning is extended at the onset of the class meeting via the opening day PowerPoint presentation. Designed like an actual invitation, the initial slide provides a springboard into the first day.

Upon extending the invitation for learning, active learning strategies such as a think-pair-share lead to a grand conversation (whole-group discussion) about personal and social responsibility among members of the learning community. The social context of learning takes center stage. Emphasis is placed on creating a shared vision and common goals that foster collegiality among the learning community. Collectively, the group sets clear expectations for how each person can contribute to the shared learning experience in the context of the course at either the undergraduate or graduate level.

Another key element fundamental to the first day is developing a positive rapport with learners and among the learning community. The intentionality of the design of the first day fosters powerful interactions designed to strengthen faculty and student relationships. Similarly, this environment becomes a model for preservice teachers to use to foster positive adult-child relationships in their practice.

"Getting to know you" activities and icebreakers support community building all the while fostering playful, active learning. For example, National Rubber Duck Day is celebrated in January. The theme of the first day of the spring semester revolves around the novelty of this celebration while simultaneously laying the foundation for the coursework. Learners reflect on their childhood memories associated with rubber ducks while getting acquainted with their new classmates. Rubber ducks are utilized as a playful prop to assign collaborative groups. Students are invited to engage as playmakers within these groups to make connections with resources provided, demonstrating how rubber ducks can promote playful learning in the early childhood classroom.

The impact of the overall experience of the first day creates a sense of belonging, trust, and warmth within the learning environment. This feeling of contentment enriches the "hygge" of the learning community. The quality of hygge is strongly aligned with Project Zero's pedagogy of play research. Hygge is a quality in the Danish culture that embodies a feeling of contentment and a sense of warmth as a result of an experience (English Oxford Living Dictionaries, s.v. "hygge"). The impact of the first day leaves an impression on the students, which inspires them to create their own such environment in their own classrooms. The first day sets the tone for the semester: hence, the mise en place (Weisberg, Hirsh-Pasek, Michnick Golinkoff, & McCandliss, 2014). Putting key ingredients in place on the first day helps cultivate a rich, meaningful, playful learning environment that promotes overall growth and development of the learners (Hassinger-Das, Hirsh-Pasek, & Michnick Golinkoff, 2017, p. 48).

The information gathered from the first day activities is utilized to connect to learners' prior knowledge and experiences, differentiate instruction, and promote ongoing positive interactions over the course of the semester. At the culmination of the first day, learners are encouraged to RSVP to the invitation for learning. Upon acceptance of this invitation, learners share something they hope to learn over the course of the semester. Learners place sticky notes with their RSVP to the invitation and their hopes for the semester on the board as they exit class.

Element 2. Engaging with Course Material

The next element of the pattern of practice promotes students' active engagement in learning to gain a deeper understanding of course content. A hands-on, minds-on approach is emphasized. This teacher educator employs a few specific active learning strategies that provide opportunities for the learners to engage with course readings. Learners take ownership of reading by actively participating in literature circles and Project Zero's thinking routines (link included in Recommended Resources). These active learning strategies promote critical thinking and a deeper understanding of the course content. Literature circles empower the learners to connect and engage with course readings through assigned roles such as questioner, illustrator, connector, investigator, and literary luminary. Each member of the literature circle demonstrates personal accountability to their group. Small-group conversations lead into a grand conversation supporting meaning-making of learner engagement with course content. Literature circle roles rotate weekly.

A hands-on, minds-on approach toward engagement with course content involves recreating a playful learning environment that fosters the curious nature of young children. The environment is prepared to promote playful, active learning. The learners actively engage with materials through play, discovery, exploration, and tinkering. Materials may include play-doh, puppets, loose parts, blocks, children's literature, paints, and dramatic play props, to name a few. Course content explored playfully includes topics such as learning through play, developmentally appropriate practice, strategies to enhance student motivation and engagement, creating, loose parts, social-emotional development, and creating a culture of inquiry integrating science and literacy in pre-K–4 learning environments. Scaffolding learning to support a deeper understanding of course material is often extended *beyond the walls of the classroom.*

Element 3. Extending the Learning Community:
Learning Inside and Outside Room 229

Working in a metropolitan area, this teacher educator seeks opportunities to extend learning by encouraging direct engagement with the rich resources in the city. Authentic learning is bringing the curriculum to life and reinforcing a hands-on, minds-on approach to learning. Opening the door and welcoming learning opportunities beyond the four walls of Room 229 is integral to the overall growth and development of the learning community. Preservice teachers need to engage in real-world learning experiences. The learners have an opportunity to see firsthand theory coming to life in practice.

Explorations beyond the classroom have included adventures to the following places:

- On-campus early learning center
- Innovation Factory (campus makerspace)
- Art museum on campus
- A nearby nature preschool
- Please Touch Museum
- Historic Smith Memorial Playground
- Headquarters for a former NAEYC affiliate

Learners deepened their understanding of high-quality early learning environments, developmentally appropriate practice, advocacy in the field of early childhood, the value of play in early learning, and the significance of the development of the whole child.

Enriched, meaningful learning experiences within the class are inclusive of visits from local early childhood teachers and advocates. An example is a representative from the mayor's Office of Education who discusses the implications of the sweetened beverage tax and its impact on early care and education in the city. Central to extending our learning opportunities is the documentation of these learning experiences. This leads us to the next integral element of the pattern of practice, which is documentation.

Element 4. Documenting Learning: The Role of Class Historian

Vital to the pattern of practice is documenting shared learning experiences, reflecting on past actions, and making connections to future learning. The role of class historian does just that. Over the course of the semester, each learner is assigned a class meeting to act as the class historian in which they document the shared learning experience through photos, video, and anecdotal notes. The class historian captures the details of our shared learning experience and recreates the experience in a presentation to share at the start of the subsequent class meeting. From the first day of the semester, an emphasis is placed on how the learning community creates a rich, vivid story just waiting to be told. Our learning community is creating the story and making history together. Textbox 6.1 shows the class historian assignment guidelines.

The role of the class historian is multifaceted in nature and showcases the intricacies of the teaching and learning process. First, the presentation shared at the start of class provides an opportunity to review past learning, highlight key concepts and content explored, align learning experiences with student learning outcomes, design exam questions, and entice the learning community with a provocation connecting to the new content. Next, a module on Canvas (the course learning management system) is created as a gathering place for the class historian presentations.

These summaries provide valuable evidence to support the teaching and learning cycle in our learning community. The students learn from each other by recognizing connections between their experiences as well as pinpointing disconnects with course content that may occur. The collection of summaries supports review and preparation for the midterm examination, which includes questions posed in the class historian presentations.

TEXTBOX 6.1. CLASS HISTORIAN ASSIGNMENT GUIDELINES—MAKING LEARNING VISIBLE

Reflecting on past actions is an essential propensity of learning community members. This collection will provide us an opportunity to reflect upon our growth and development as engaged learners over the course of the semester.

The class historian will *capture* and *document* the **process** of teaching and learning during our weekly shared learning experiences. The role of class historian is significant to our professional growth as educators. This documentation will provide valuable evidence to support the teaching and learning cycle in our learning community. The documentation will help our learning community see clear connections between our experiences as well as pinpoint disconnects that may occur in our learning.

Presentation/Documentation Essential Elements:

- Capture the *key ideas*, *concepts*, and *happenings* during our time together. Your recollection will lead to a deeper understanding of course content for us.
- Evidence and artifacts include snapshots/video clips and anecdotes.
- A creative element including a theme for the presentation as a result of your reflection is evident.
- Provide a link to course learning outcomes per the course syllabus.
- Develop three exam questions spanning Bloom's taxonomy (lower level–higher level).
- Tap into your curiosity quotient. Include one additional resource to extend learning.
- Pose a *provocation* leading into the next topic and/or reading.
- The presentation is due on the *Sunday or Thursday evening (8:00 pm)* before you present.

Theory to Practice:

- **Observation/Documentation:** Documentation Board/Panel (Utilize a *technological tool* to create your presentation.)
  - Learning is documented from the beginning to the end of the endeavor
  - Snapshot/anecdote/brief narrative related to learning objective

- **Information Processing Theory: "COVER"-ing the content through a deeper, more meaningful learning experience**
  - **C – Connect to prior knowledge**
  - **O – Organize the material presented**
  - **V – Visuals to represent material**
  - **ER – Elaborative Rehearsal—Practice and review with feedback**

- **Provocation:** Provocations provoke. . . . They provoke thoughts, discussions, questions, interests, creativity, and ideas. They can also *expand* on a thought, project, idea, or interest. Ultimately, the intention of provocations is to provide an invitation for a learner to explore and express themselves. It should be *open-ended* and provide a means for *expression* where possible.

The role of class historian fosters a creative flair and contributes to the playful active learning environment. The historian chooses a theme to capture the essence of the presentation. The presentations allow for the visibility of what was learned over the course of the semester. Lastly, the role of class historian provides authentic practice of powerful assessment strategies in early childhood inclusive of observation and documentation.

Element 5. Embracing the Joy of the Profession: The Last Day of Class

Equally important to the first day of class is the last day of class. The last day of class honors and celebrates the accomplishments of the learning community, marking the end of our journey together. Simultaneously, it paves the transition for each member of the learning community toward their own journey forward. This teacher educator carefully crafts the culmination of the semester as a celebration of the successes and recognition of failures having shaped our shared learning experiences. Each semester ends with a playful active learning experience designed to embrace the joy of the profession. Examples include the following:

- games
- sharing a portfolio of pictures and artifacts
- reflective writing, including a self-portrait with sticky note glasses titled "I can see clearly now . . ."
- graduation party (celebrating our senior preservice teachers)
- baby shower
- Red Nose Day or other novel learning experiences

Specifically, games like Jeopardy (online) and Candyland are played to review course content aligned with student learning outcomes. The baby-shower-themed culmination of the course titled "Foundations of Early Childhood Education" was in celebration of two classmates who were expecting. Learners played baby shower games reflecting on the overall learning experience and course content aligned with student learning outcomes. Another culminating experience celebrated Red Nose Day (a campaign sponsored by Comic Relief Inc. in May dedicated to ending child poverty), which reinforces the learners' role as advocates in the field of early care and education. This culminating experience was directly aligned with a course assignment titled "Investigate, Report, and Advocacy Project." The final class meeting is designed as an affirmation and validation of *hygge* within the learning community.

Element 6. Engaging in Reflective Practice

The end of the semester is marked by reflective practice. Hence, the last element of the pattern of practice is threaded together. One example of reflective practice includes analyzing course evaluations. This analysis assists the teacher educator in pinpointing strengths and areas for potential growth. Revisiting the class historian projects provides another opportunity to see the story that unfolded over the course of the semester. Engaging in reflection provides insight to inform future practice, strengthening the fabric of a playful, active learning community.

OUTCOMES LINKED TO THE PATTERN OF PRACTICE

Formative assessments provide an ongoing understanding of the learners' grasp of content knowledge and skill application. Many of the formative assessments employed over the course of the semester include games, reflections, quizzes, grand conversations, and the class historian summaries. Yet this teacher educator discovered that a more accurate assessment of the impact of the pattern of practice promoting playful, active learning was needed. Measuring transformational learning linked directly to a pattern of practice promoting playful, active learning in specific performance assessments is a challenge.

The impact of the pattern of practice promoting playful, active learning became visible through anecdotal feedback from student responses on the course evaluation at the end of the semester. Two themes that emerged were clear descriptions of students feeling engaged in the activities and enthusiastic about learning. These outcomes are the essence of hygge (discussed earlier in the chapter).

LESSONS LEARNED

Engaging in Reflective Practice on the Pattern of Practice

Engaging in reflective practice is instrumental to the growth of a learning community for both students and instructors alike. Strengths and areas for growth potential are identified before *repeating* the pattern of practice for the upcoming semester. Both positive and negative feedback are internalized to fine-tune elements of the pattern of practice. Analyzing outcomes identified by students associated with the overall impact of the pattern of practice illuminates areas for growth.

One lesson learned was the need to be more explicit about my practice. The challenge in creating a playful learning environment is modeling "fun" as an approach to learning but also having students recognize where and how that learning is also rigorous and critical. Clarity and transparency about the intended goals of the learning environment, which are implicit by the nature of being playful, must then be explicitly stated to students during class discussions.

Hence, we should practice what we preach. This can be achieved by adapting the invitation extended to the learners on the first day of class. Invite learners to share in a joint venture of playful, active learning. The class can begin to unpack what this might look, sound, and feel like, followed by a conversation on professional preparation as meaning-making. Furthermore, there is a need to include playful active learning as an indicator for assessing student work where appropriate.

Another lesson learned reinforces the need for the teacher educator to take risks in practice to support both professional growth and the overall growth of the learners. "Making room for playful learning in school can be difficult. Formidable tensions exist between playful learning and the way pedagogy is currently structured in most schools" (Mardell et al., 2016, p. 2).

Modeling risk-taking is integral to the growth of a learning community, which promotes a growth mindset. Teacher educators must be willing to model risk-taking by using innovative pedagogies and failures to inform future success and build character within learners.

Preservice teachers need to see themselves as lifelong learners advocating for playful, active learning. The lessons learned provide food for thought for other teacher educators as they craft a "pattern of practice." The pattern of practice can be differentiated in accordance with the nuances and intricacies of one's context, content, and most importantly, the learners. The impact of the pattern of practice shared in this chapter results from the synergistic effect of all six elements threaded throughout course design, creating the fabric of a playful, active learning community.

RECOMMENDED RESOURCES

The collection of recommended resources listed below can be utilized to fashion course design to reflect a pattern of practice supporting the fabric of a playful, active learning community. These resources help frame the pattern of practice designed by this teacher educator and shared in this chapter. Engaging in an exploration of these resources and joining or initiating a professional learning community may entice curious, playful early childhood teacher educators to seek ways to enhance or create a pattern of practice, ultimately strengthening the fabric of a playful, active learning community.

Books

Drew, W. F. (2013). *From play to practice—connecting teachers' play to children's learning.* Washington, DC: National Association for the Education of Young Children.

Epstein, A. S. (2014). *The intentional teacher: Choosing the best strategies for young children's learning* (Rev. ed.). Washington, DC: National Association for the Education of Young Children.

Sheridan, R. (2015). *Joy, Inc.: How we built a workplace people love.* New York: Portfolio/Penguin.

Articles

Baker, M., Krechevsky, M., Ertel, K., Ryan, J., Wilson, D., & Mardell, B. (2016). Playful participatory research: An emerging methodology for developing a pedagogy of play. Project Zero.

The influence on playful learning for adults. (2018). Retrieved from http://www.pz.harvard.edu/sites/default/files/Staff%20meeting%20PoP%20PoP.pdf

Weisberg, D. S., Hirsh-Pasek, K., Golinkoff, R. M., & McCandliss, B. D. (2014). Mise en place: Setting the stage for thought and action. *Trends in Cognitive Sciences, 18*(6), 276–278.

Websites

Center for Research on Learning and Teaching, University of Michigan. Retrieved from http://www.crlt.umich.edu/active_learning_introduction

Project Zero, Harvard Graduate School of Education—Pedagogy of Play. Retrieved from http://www.pz.harvard.edu/projects/pedagogy-of-play

Project Zero, Harvard Graduate School of Education—Visible Thinking. Retrieved from http://www.pz.harvard.edu/projects/visible-thinking

US Play Coalition. Retrieved from https://usplaycoalition.org/

Play Study Group: National Association of Early Childhood Teacher Educators. Retrieved from https://www.naeyc.org/resources/pubs/yc/nov2018/inquiry-is-play-playful-participatory-research.

ResearchNet: Exploring Creativity and Play in Early Childhood Teacher Education. Retrieved from https://naecte.org/about/researchnets/.

BIBLIOGRAPHY

Baker, Megina, Krechevsky, Mara, Ertel, Katie, Ryan, Jen, Wilson, Daniel, & Mardell, Ben. (2016). Playful participatory research: An emerging methodology for developing a pedagogy of play. Project Zero.

English Oxford Living Dictionaries, s.v. "hygge." Retrieved from https://en.oxforddictionaries.com/definition/hygge

Hassinger-Das, Brenna, Hirsh-Pasek, Kathy, & Michnick Golinkoff, Roberta. (2017). The case of brain science and guided play. *YC Young Children, 72*(2), 45–50.

Mardell, Ben, Wilson, Daniel, Ryan, Jen, Krechevsky, Mara, Ertel, Katie, & Baker, Megina. (2016). Towards a pedagogy of play. Project Zero.

Merriam Webster, s.v. "pattern." Retrieved from https://www.merriam-webster.com/dictionary/pattern

National Association for the Education of Young Children. (2009). *NAEYC standards for early childhood professional preparation: A position statement of the National Association for the Education of Young Children.* Washington, DC: NAEYC.

Weisberg, Deena Skolnick, Hirsh-Pasek, Kathy, Michnick Golinkoff, Roberta, & McCandliss, Bruce D. (2014). Mise en place: Setting the stage for thought and action. *Trends in Cognitive Sciences, 18*(6), 276–278.

Chapter Seven

Professional Learning Communities from the Inside Out

Teacher Candidates' Perceptions and Experiences

Jill A. Smith

Preparing preservice teacher (PST) candidates for a smooth, successful transition to public, private, or charter school community environments is one of the most critical responsibilities of a university-level professional education division. Identifying and addressing the dissimilarities between the sterile environment of the university classroom and the real-life challenges of public school life can be overwhelming for first-year teachers. Along with content-specific knowledge, developmental and educational psychology, pedagogy and professional ethics, preparing PSTs to work collaboratively within a community of teachers and other education professionals is essential to their successful transition to the teaching profession.

Currently, many public, private, and charter schools support a practice whereby teachers and other education professionals work together in professional learning communities (PLCs) in order to promote effective practices within their teaching faculty. PLCs foster successful teaching methods such as reflective dialogue, de-privatization of teaching practices, a collective focus on student learning, collaboration among teaching professionals, and shared norms and values (DuFour, DuFour, Eaker, & Many, 2013).

PSTs become better equipped to develop and communicate their individual knowledge, together with a greater collective wisdom, when they are given opportunities for collaborative inquiry and reflective learning associated with university-level course assignments. Teacher educators, who expand their goals for preparing future teachers to include a focus on effective participation within collaborative learning teams, help bridge the transition from teacher education programs to the actual teaching profession.

Learning to interact successfully within a community of educational professionals is a part of the course work necessary to fulfill the requirements of the education major's degree plan. Research suggests that collaborative school cultures in which teacher development is facilitated through reciprocal support, shared investigation, and collective agreement on educational values seem the best settings for maximizing student achievement (Gruenert, 2005). Teachers gain information about, and reasoning for, participation in PLCs, as well as specific strategies for effective participation within the school community, through carefully designed upper-level courses that are within the education major degree coursework. A professional learning community can be defined as educators committed to working collaboratively in an ongoing process of collective inquiry and action research to achieve better results for the students they serve (DuFour, DuFour, Eaker, & Many, 2008).

The theory behind PLCs suggests that in order to make a significant difference in improving student learning, teachers must engage in frequent and relevant professional development. Building collaborative teams of teachers within schools is the foundational cornerstone of successful PLCs—collaborative teams whose members work *interdependently* to achieve *common goals*; goals that are linked to the purpose of *learning for all* and for which members are held *mutually accountable*. PSTs who participate in collaborative and interdependent teams that collaboratively and interdependently complete assignments and projects before engaging within a community of professional educators will ultimately be better prepared to participate in PLCs once they enter the profession.

IMPLEMENTATION EXAMPLE BASED ON AN UNDERGRADUATE COURSE

On the first day of class, students complete a pre-course survey designed to determine PSTs' knowledge, attitudes, beliefs, and experiences with PLCs prior to taking the course. Some examples of questions include the following:

- "I believe there is value in collaborating with others to complete course assignments,"
- "I am stimulated to higher levels of thinking and inspired to work harder when I work with others in a team,"
- "I believe I learn more when I discuss course content with other students,"
- "I become conflicted and distracted when working with others in a team," and

- "I believe collaborating with a team builds collective knowledge, and therefore strengthens students' learning."

This provides a baseline for changes throughout the semester as a result of participating in the course readings, teamwork assignments, team discussions, self-reflection, practicum visits, and observations of PLCs in action.

During the second class meeting, the professor presents and explains knowledge concerning the historical origins, research-based practices, and practical application of PLCs in public schools today. A distinct difference between "group" interactions and assignments and "team" interactions and assignments is thoroughly clarified. After providing PSTs with a foundation of knowledge concerning the rationale for PLCs in the education workplace, the professor launches candidates on a journey toward understanding the role of professional learning teams (PLTs) as a vital part of their teacher preparation program. The professor explains that PLTs are a prototype of PLCs that will be implemented during the course as a means of preparing PSTs for their participation in PLCs once they accept a position as a professional educator in a public, private, or charter school. While one full class period (2 hours and 50 minutes) is devoted to introducing candidates to PLCs, the content and application of PLCs are woven into the remaining course work and content.

Once PST candidates have a basic understanding of PLCs and their participation in PLTs as a part of the course, they are divided into three-, four-, or five-member teams (depending on the number of students in the class) through a process of random assignment. Random assignment is used to assign PSTs to teams due to its correlation to the real world of educational institutions, where teaching faculty do not have a choice of colleagues with whom to work on a grade-level team.

Two necessary first steps in turning groups into effective teams involve setting forth a clear set of guidelines for team functioning and having team members formulate a common set of expectations for one another (Oakley, Felder, Brent, & Elhajj, 2004). Candidates are subsequently educated on effective *team* interactions as well as procedures and methods for assigning team member roles and responsibilities. Team members negotiate, establish, and clarify the duties of each role, including facilitator, record keeper, time keeper, and coordinator. From that time forward, candidates meet in teams to jointly complete assignments required in the course.

For teams to effectively function as "high-performance learning teams" (Fink, 2004), the professor intentionally makes teamwork the *primary* strategy for completing assignments. Time in class is provided for teams to meet and plan work; carefully structured activities promote active interdependent learning. The professor designs assignments that challenge PSTs and then provides adequate feedback upon completion of assignments as a guide for future course expectations. Assignments require preservice teachers to collectively and interdependently develop and participate in 1) an integrated study (thematic unit); 2) collaboratively designed cross-disciplinary lesson plans related to the integrated study; 3) clinical practicum visits in a public school classroom (each team member partners with one other member from the team), where they implement the lesson plans collaboratively designed by their team; 4) reflection on their experiences in public school classrooms and the effectiveness of the lesson plan when implemented; and 5) collective team PowerPoints on prominent learning theorists and community-based educational programs.

Team members self-evaluate their own performances as well as the performances of each of their fellow team members. Scores on a self-evaluation rubric, as well as a team-evaluation rubric, are included as a part of each student's final grade. Using points based on a Likert scale, the rubrics measure the extent to which individual members and the team meet two criteria: 1) working collaboratively and interdependently with others; and 2) fulfilling their expected role on the team, including sharing in the workload, decision making, and motivating others.

The assignment of most significant importance involves each PLT designing an integrated study. The components of the integrated study assigned to individual teams include the following: 1) Title Page and Table of Contents; 2) Study Rationale; 3) Essential Understandings; 4) Guiding Questions; 5) Graphic Organizer (Thematic Curriculum Planning Web); 6) Planning Guide and Schedule; 7) Final Project; and 8) References. All team members are responsible for ensuring proper formatting and grammar of the final project.

The class as a whole collectively brainstorms integrated study topics. An anchor chart listing possible topics is developed, from which individual teams select their integrated study theme. With the thematic topic as a starting point, each team uses a thematic curriculum planning web to design an integrated curriculum unit covering all content areas, as well as the arts, snacks/nutrition, technology, physical activity, and outdoor play around the integrated study topic for a theme. As a part of planning to implement the integrated study, a set of four thematically integrated, cross-curricular lesson plans are designed. Each of the four lesson plans includes two cross-curricular lesson objectives.

For an integrated study theme of *Forests*, team members collectively design four lesson plans for early primary grade students. Sample objectives for lesson plans might include the following:

- The students create a picture of a leaf man based on the book *Leaf Man* by Lois Ehlert, using real leaves and each orally telling a story about the activities of their leaf men (art and language objective).

- The students create simple patterns using two or three types of leaf impressions cast in play-doh (art, math, and science objective).
- After reading the story *Where Once There Was a Wood* by Denise Fleming, the students take a nature walk on the school playground and take photographs of the trees they observe (language arts and science objective).
- The students design a simple map of the location and identify the types of trees on the school playground (social studies and science objective).
- After reading the story *A Walk Through the Woods* by Helen Musselwhite and Louise Greig, the students draw a picture of their favorite forest animal from the story (art and language arts objective).

Along with seated class time during the course, PSTs complete a clinical field experience. Working together with one of their team partners, PSTs complete five visits to a local cooperating public school classroom (grades kindergarten through third grade). While four out of five of the clinical visits involve mainly observation and interactions with the students in the classroom, during at least one of the visits PSTs implement one of the four integrated lesson plans designed by the team.

At the conclusion of each clinical visit, PSTs write a reflection on the clinical visit. Reflections are written in a format that includes a describe section, an analyze section, and a plan section. These assignments are turned in and receive points that count toward each candidate's grade. PSTs write about what the children in the classrooms do and say; what they (the PSTs) do with and say to the children as they interact; and what the teacher says and does during their visits to the classroom. The emphasis for the reflections is on the children and the PSTs as future teachers. Reflections never critique the cooperating teachers' performance.

At midterm of the clinical field experience, the teams collectively meet to discuss their experiences during the field experience placements and while observing their cooperating teachers, and to discuss what they believe are their individual strengths and struggles as preservice teachers during clinical visits to the public school classrooms. A class period is designated for this collective discussion.

Each PST completes an individual reflection plan (IRP) in preparation for the team discussion. The purpose of the IRP is to have individual team members reflect on their experiences during the practicum field experiences and then process these trials and triumphs with their team members. As PST team members meet together, they share their personal successes and challenges and mentor one another. The team as a whole responds to each team member and completes the team discussion brief (TDB), which is turned in to the professor at the end of the class period. These reflective TDBs serve as a window into the thoughts and experiences of individual PSTs and allow the professor to view the mentoring skills of the team as a whole.

In addition to the integrated study and the lesson plan design assignments, candidates work together in interdependent teams to complete team presentations on educational theorists (five of the most well-known educational theorists) and community-based programs (programs in the community that provide locations for quality educational field trips, as well as teacher and family resources). Grades on these two assignments are based on a "team score" of a collaboratively designed PowerPoint presentation. The incentive to work together is fostered by the understanding that the more collaboratively and interdependently the students work together, the more likely their work produces high-quality content, leading to a higher grade on the presentation.

The theory behind the *team* grade is modeled after one of the goals of PLCs: "A PLC is composed of collaborative teams whose members work interdependently to achieve common goals—goals linked to the purpose of learning for all—for which members are held mutually accountable" (DuFour, DuFour, Eaker, & Many, 2008, p. 15). Each team member brings particular strengths to the team, and the team is codependent on the strengths of each team member. By collaborating on the assignments, each team member contributes the highest level of expertise toward a common goal (i.e., the assignment) for which all team members are accountable. When the team as a whole benefits from individual team members' strengths, it serves to inspire higher levels of commitment from each of the team members.

Between midterm and the end of the course, the professor arranges for a class field trip to a nearby public elementary school that practices PLCs regularly so students can witness grade-level teachers engaged in a PLC data-team meeting. In the best-case scenario, the visit begins with the principal explaining the rationale for, and value of, PLC data-team meetings as an instrument for improving student achievement, overall school improvement, and professional development of teachers. Student data (e.g., literacy running record scores given on a biweekly or monthly basis, developmental reading assessments, benchmark scores collected at the beginning of the year and the middle of the school year, etc.) are displayed.

When possible, the principal agrees to explain how the PLC teams analyze assessment data to monitor students' progress in reading and math as well as to compare and contrast the effectiveness of teaching practices. Through this process, teachers identify the most effective learning activities and instructional methods. Ideally, PSTs witness a discussion between the principal and teachers, as well as discussion among the PLC team members as they analyze and evaluate test score data, as well as students' assignments and progress on particular curricular content. The purpose of the discussion among teachers is to identify for future implementation those activities, experiences, and instructional strategies that result in the best student learning and test scores.

After each semester, PSTs are resurveyed on the same set of questions from the beginning of the class. Additionally, PSTs are invited to participate in a focus group interview, conducted at the end of the course by an objective colleague (another professor in the education division), who does not teach the same course. Focus group questions are open ended and encourage discussion among the interviewees. Some examples relevant to the course objectives learned over the semester include, "What aspects of working in PLTs did you find effective? What aspects would you improve upon? How? Overall, how would you describe your experiences working with PLTs?" The PSTs' responses to pre- and post-surveys, together with transcriptions of the focus group interviews, are reviewed by the professor and used to learn more about how best to meet learning objectives for the course in the future.

CHALLENGES IMPLEMENTING PLCS IN UNDERGRADUATE COURSES

PLTs may have little to no prior knowledge of PLCs. Introduction to PLCs must include the history, purpose, and inner workings of PLCs as a base of knowledge on which to build a hands-on application. Additionally, a culture of independent learning pervades the majority of PLTs' learning experiences in elementary, middle, and high school. Due to these prior experiences, working in collaborative teams is abnormal to their expectations for completing assignments and receiving an evaluation of their work.

PLTs may prefer to work independently rather than collaboratively and interdependently in PLCs. It takes time to change deeply entrenched cultural norms of behavior in university classrooms. Based on this potential challenge, the earlier PSTs can be introduced to the concept of, and expectation for, teamwork as a viable alternative to independent completion of assignments in their professional education coursework, the greater the chance that PSTs may learn to value this method of collaborative and interdependent learning.

Another potential challenge encountered in implementing PLTs as a learning strategy involves fair evaluation of students' performance on teams. When PSTs participate on a team, they traditionally have inflated perceptions of their value and performance as team members. This view is often not shared by the other members of the team. Since self-evaluation, as well as peer evaluation, should be valued equally, the professor needs to put some measures in place to ensure a more credible view of individual team member's contributions. Clearly conveying the guidelines for promoting effective teamwork early on, as well as intentionally outlining the roles and responsibilities for each team member, goes a long way toward heading off potentially inflated self-perceptions. Also, checking in frequently with teams throughout the semester, as well as having PSTs thoughtfully and frequently reflect on their performances, may increase accuracy in team members' evaluations of self and peers on the team.

PSTs prefer selecting their own team members. It is important to introduce PSTs to the reality that public, private, and charter school PLC teams are generally composed based on grade-level groupings and that random team assignment better replicates reality in public schools. Social loafing (a phenomenon where team members allow/expect other members of the team to do their work) within teams is another concern for PSTs. Alerting students to the potential pitfalls of this problem and equipping them with suggestions for confronting those students in a professional manner teaches PSTs strategies for confronting the occurrence when it arises.

Another reasons PSTs do not like completing assignments in groups is due to meeting with groups outside of class (Fink, 2004). This is especially challenging for students who commute or are involved in multiple extracurricular activities. Setting aside time during class for teams to meet makes teamwork more appealing for those who have negative attitudes about, and negative past experiences with, teamwork.

A final challenge needing accommodation is that PSTs have concerns about team members' absenteeism and members who lack investment in the learning process; they worry about team members who have a checklist approach to learning versus building team knowledge and excellence of performance on the assignments. These concerns mirror those faced by grade-level teachers in many schools. Encouraging team member support improves the potential effectiveness of the team as a whole.

CONCLUSIONS

Implementing PLTs in undergraduate teacher education courses is an impactful practice that contributes to PSTs' preparation to work collaboratively within a community of teachers and with other education professionals. Expanding goals for the professional preparation of future teachers, to include effective participation in interdependent learning teams, helps bridge the transition between the primarily independent completion of most university course assignments and the collective development of instructional activities and implementation strategies by PLCs in public schools. This practice facilitates the transition from teacher preparation programs to the professional teaching community.

BIBLIOGRAPHY

Danielson, Charlotte. (1996). *Enhancing professional practice: A framework for teaching.* Alexandria, VA: ASCD.

Drago-Severson, Eleanor. (2004). *Helping teachers learn: Principal leadership for adult and school.* Washington, DC: National Academy Press.

DuFour, Robert, DuFour, Rebecca, Eaker, Robert, & Many, Thomas. (2013). *Learning by doing: A handbook for professional learning communities at work* (2nd ed.). Bloomington, IN: Solution Tree Press.

DuFour, Robert, DuFour, Rebecca, Eaker, Robert, & Many, Thomas. (2008). *Revisiting professional learning communities at work: New insights for improving schools.* Bloomington, IN: Solution Tree Press.

DuFour, Robert, DuFour, Rebecca, & Eaker, Robert (Eds.). (2005). *On common ground: The power of professional learning communities.* Bloomington, IN: Solution Tree Press.

Fink, L. Dee. (2004). Beyond small groups: Harnessing the extraordinary power of learning teams. In L. K. Michaelsen, A. B. Knight, and L. D. Fink (eds.), *Team-based learning: A transformative use of small groups in college teaching.* Sterling, VA: Stylus Publishing, 3–26.

Fullan, Michael. (2001). *Leading in a culture of change.* San Francisco: Jossey-Bass.

Gruenert, Steve. (2005). Correlations of collaborative school cultures with student achievement. *NASSP Bulletin,* 89(645), 43–55.

Hord, Shirley M. (2004). Professional learning communities: An overview. In S. M. Hord (ed.), *Learning together, leading together: Changing schools through professional learning communities.* New York: Teachers College Press, 5–14.

Kruse, Sharon D. (1997). Reflective activity in practice: Vignettes of teachers' deliberative work. *Journal of Research and Development in Education,* 31(1), 46–60.

Lieberman, Ann, & Miller, Lynne (Eds.). (2001). *Teachers caught in the action: Professional development that matters.* New York: Teachers College Press.

McLaughlin, Milbrey Wallin, & Talbert, Joan E. (2006). *Building school-based learning communities: Professional strategies to improve student achievement.* New York: Teachers College Press.

Novick, Bernard, Kress, Jeffrey S., & Elias, Maurice J. (2002). *Building learning communities with character.* Alexandria, VA: ASCD.

Oakley, Barbara, Felder, Richard M., Brent, Rebecca, & Elhajj, Imad H. (2004). Turning student groups into effective teams. *Journal of Student Centered Learning,* 2(1), 9–34.

Oakley, Barbara. (2002). How "good" students enable problematic behavior in teams. *Journal of Student Centered Learning,* 1(1), 19–27.

Perret-Clairmont, Anne-Nelly, Perret, Jean-François, & Bell, Nancy (1991). The social construction of meaningful cognitive activity in elementary school children. In S. D. Teasely & L. B. Resnick (eds.), *Perspectives on socially shared cognition.* Washington, DC: American Psychological Association, 41–62.

Servage, Laura. (2008). Critical and transformative practices in professional learning communities. *Teacher Education Quarterly,* 35(1), 63–77.

Stoll, Louise, Bolam, Ray, McMahon, Agnes, Wallace, Mike, & Thomas, Salley. (2006). Professional learning communities: A review of the literature. *Journal of Educational Change,* 7(4), 221–258.

Vygotsky, L. S. (1978). *Mind in society: The development of higher mental processes* (M. Cole, trans.). Cambridge, MA: Harvard University Press.

Wheelen, Susan. (2005). *Faculty groups: From frustration to collaboration.* Thousand Oaks, CA: Corwin Press.

Part II

Innovation in Curriculum and Instruction

Chapter Eight

Hydroponic Gardens as a Learning Tool with Preservice Teachers

Louise Ammentorp

In the last few years, the field of early childhood education has experienced an exciting shift toward embracing outdoor and nature-based learning experiences. Organizations such as Natural Start Alliance and Children & Nature Network lead the charge on the importance of nature-based learning for young children. Recent research from the North American Association for Environmental Education (NAAEE, 2017a) confirms the benefits of environmental education for learners in K–12 settings, including improving academic performance, enhancing critical thinking skills, and developing personal growth, life building skills, confidence, autonomy, and leadership.

Research also shows the value of exploring nature for developing the whole child—socially, emotionally, physically, cognitively, and spiritually (Kellert, 2005). For example, children involved in nature-based activities have improved self-efficacy and early literacy skills (Trent-Brown, 2011). Not surprisingly, children's connection to nature also influences the performance of environmentally friendly behaviors (Cheng & Monroe, 2012).

A recent survey by NAAEE (2017b) found there are more than 250 nature-based preschools across the United States, two-thirds more than there were in the previous year. With the emergence of nature preschools in the United States and around the globe, as well as the increasing criticism of academic pressure in early childhood classrooms, there is a clear recognition in the early childhood field of the importance of engaging children in nature-based learning.

However, in the K–3 public school context, nature-based experiences are often relegated to science instruction, and students are not getting much of it. Just 20% of K–3 students have access to daily science instruction (Blank,

2012). According to the recently revised National Science Teaching Association's Elementary Science Statement (2018), "In many schools and districts, however, elementary science instruction often takes a back seat to math and reading and receives little time in the school day. Many elementary educators do not receive an adequate amount of professional learning to gain the confidence needed to teach science" (Horizon Research, 2013; McClure et al., 2017).

In their clinical placements, therefore, preservice teachers may experience little science curriculum, with the increased challenge of poor quality of the curriculum to which they are exposed. This, combined with ECE preservice teachers often identifying as "non-science" people, who may not know how to integrate authentic science and nature experiences in the classroom, creates a gap in their ability to develop as educators. Teacher education programs, therefore, must maximize the opportunity to introduce high-quality, nature-based learning experiences, and not just in the science methods courses.

HYDROPONIC GARDENING BASICS AND BENEFITS

There is an abundance of evidence regarding the academic, social-emotional, and physical benefits of school gardens for children, particularly in urban settings (Rahm, 2002). However, outdoor school gardening programs can be hard to sustain due to teachers' lack of time, funding, volunteers, space, and gardening experience, particularly in urban areas (Ozer, 2007).

Hydroponic garden systems are a viable alternative. Hydroponics does not use soil. Instead, the plants grow in a mineral-rich water, with some kind of media to hold the roots (such as *Oasis* root cubes). The plants can be grown outside or indoors, using sunlight or a lighting system. There are several types of hydroponic systems, each with their pros and cons. Some people choose to build their own hydroponic gardens, or there are kits that can be purchased. *Tower gardens* (see figure 8.1) are a popular example of a vertical hydroponic garden kit used in schools.

The flexibility in the set-up of the hydroponic gardens is one of its many benefits. The system can range from relatively cheap DIY models to more expensive and more complex systems. They are simple to use and maintain, and there is a large variety of plants that can grow in the system year-round, including fruits, vegetables, flowers, herbs, and so forth.

Given the academic calendar of most schools and colleges, it can be difficult for students to experience the growth of a plant from seed to harvest, particularly during the winter months. Plants in indoor hydroponic systems have an accelerated growth rate and are not weather dependent, so are easily integrated into classes year round. Finally, they require a small amount of

Hydroponic Gardens as a Learning Tool 89

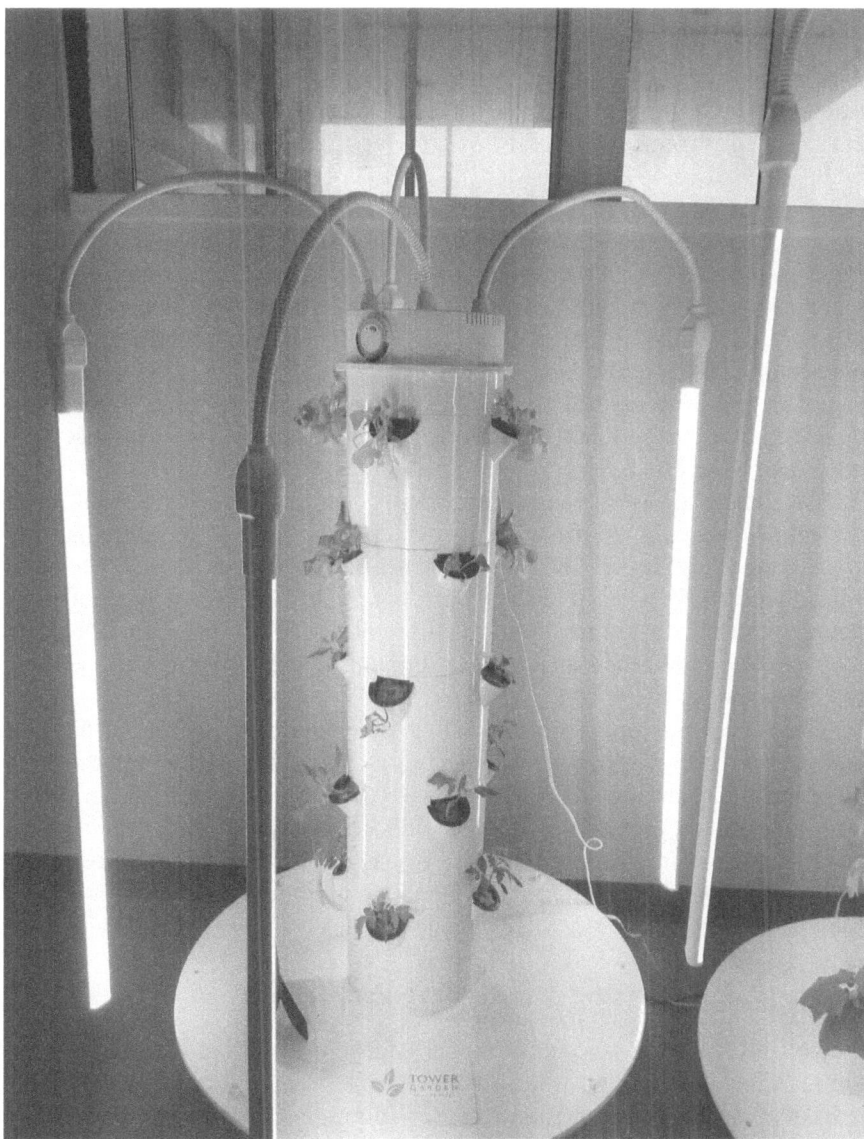

Figure 8.1. Vertical Hydroponic Garden. Photo Credit: Louise Ammentorp.

space and can be set up either indoors or outdoors. The gardens can be transformative in creating an aesthetic green space in college buildings.

IMPLEMENTATION

This chapter describes the impactful practice of using vertical hydroponic gardens as a teaching and learning tool with early childhood preservice teachers. Having the gardens in the college setting allows the students to experience for themselves the joy of growing their own fruits and vegetables while they develop the knowledge, confidence, and skills necessary for bringing authentic nature-based experiences into early childhood classrooms.

The course highlighted in this chapter is not a science methods class; rather, it is a course that focuses on instructional methods, class management, planning, assessment, and differentiation with a substantial field component of about 180 hours in the field. All early childhood (p–3 certification) and elementary (k–6 certification) majors are required to take the course the semester before student teaching. This provides an opportunity for all students to get the experience of working with the gardens, not just those who are already interested.

The course meets as a three-hour seminar on campus twice a week, with the entire class going to the same elementary school for a day and a half per week, and every day for two weeks at the end of the semester. The future educators work in pairs in the same classroom over the course of the semester. They teach weekly lessons, which are observed by their professor, and they develop and teach a two-week unit on a topic of their cooperative teacher's choosing.

The school placement for this course every spring semester for the past eight years has been Hopewell Elementary School (HES). HES won the 2018 New Jersey Department of Agriculture Best Farm to School Program. It has both an outdoor garden and a large indoor hydroponic garden that grows food for their school lunch program. This school is the inspiration for bringing hydroponics to the college classroom and provides students many opportunities to see teachers using hydroponic gardens with young children.

Teaching and Learning with Hydroponic Gardens

One of the powerful aspects of teacher education is that preservice teachers are learning as students while simultaneously developing the metacognitive skill of thinking like a teacher. Teacher educators are working on multiple levels as well, teaching content while modeling high quality, impactful teaching practices. Hydroponic gardens can influence preservice teachers' learning on multiple levels. While learning about plants and hydroponics, they are also connecting with nature and learning strategies for teaching young children.

Hydroponic gardens have the potential to teach preservice teachers a vast array of topics, including, but not limited to, the following:

- Developing standards-aligned and interdisciplinary lessons
- Instructional methods, logistical planning, class management
- Science knowledge and pedagogy: life science, iSTEM, student-led inquiry, experiential learning
- Nutrition and environmental health literacy
- Issues of food equity and access
- Social-emotional learning (SEL) development and competencies
- Community building in the classroom
- School-wide programs (e.g., farm to school initiatives)

The Great Teacher's Teach Off

One fun and effective way to teach lesson planning and instruction created by the author is the "Great Teacher's Teach Off" (GTTO) activity. Similar to the cooking show *The Great British Bake Off*, participants are given a task, a set amount of time, criteria, and constraints, and must create a solution. In this case, they have to create an interdisciplinary mini-unit consisting of three lessons using the hydroponic gardens. They work with their peer partner and focus on the grade of the students in their field placement. The lessons must be aligned to standards for that grade, which they have to find online. For example, if they are placed in a second-grade class, they may find and use the following Next Generation Science Standards (NGSS) and Common Core Literacy Standards to plan their lessons:

- 2-LS4-1. Make observations of plants and animals to compare the diversity of life in different habitats.
- 2-LS2-2. Develop a simple model that mimics the function of an animal in dispersing seeds or pollinating plants.
- 2-LS2-2. Plan and conduct an investigation to determine if plants need sunlight and water to grow.
- CCSS.ELA-LITERACY.SL.2.1. Participate in collaborative conversations with diverse partners about *grade 2 topics and texts* with peers and adults in small and larger groups.
- CCSS.ELA-LITERACY.SL.2.3. Ask and answer questions about what a speaker says in order to clarify comprehension, gather additional information, or deepen understanding of a topic or issue.
- CCSS.ELA-LITERACY.W.2.7. Participate in shared research and writing projects (e.g., read a number of books on a single topic to produce a report; record science observations).
- CCSS.ELA-LITERACY.W.2.8. Recall information from experiences or gather information from provided sources to answer a question.

For the GTTO activity, the students have 30 minutes to work on their laptops and then upload their mini-unit plan to a template on Google Drive. After the 30 minutes, they share what they have created. This activity works best if they have had some experience teaching and lesson planning, but it can certainly be adapted. This activity is effective in helping them find and use standards, plan lessons collaboratively, and see the many ways that the hydroponic gardens can be used in their teaching.

In addition to life science, there are iSTEM possibilities in using the hydroponic gardens. For example, students (children and preservice teachers) can design and build simple or more complex hydroponic systems. To maintain the gardens, pH levels need to be observed, documented, and adjusted. Math concepts and skills such as numeracy, comparing, measuring, and graphing can be taught with the gardens. Language arts can be incorporated through books about gardens, writing recipe books, creating stories of plant's growth, and so forth. There are many opportunities to integrate the arts by exploring and discovering the textures, colors, and patterns of nature.

The ability to take an interdisciplinary, experiential approach to teaching and learning and see how it aligns with standards is an impactful practice for students. They are concerned with their ability to meet the standards and other requirements of teaching in the "real world," while still doing fun, engaging activities.

Modeling Discovery, Student-Led Inquiry, and Experiential Learning

Central to high-quality ECE science instruction is experiential, hands-on learning and student-led inquiry. One way to model this approach with preservice teachers is through creating observation packets for the gardens. The science packets can include guided questions, prompts and areas for questions, and sketching, similar to what they could create for their own students.

One thing that preservice teachers often struggle with is the inclination to explain or give answers to their students prematurely or correct children's misconceptions immediately. Using the hydroponic gardens in the classroom is a useful tool for modeling authentic inquiry. For example, the plants grow from seed to seedling to plant, some grow faster than others, and some don't sprout at all. The preservice teachers notice this, and start asking the instructor the cause—if it is the water, minerals, placement of the lights, the shape of the vertical garden, the type of plant, and so forth.

This is such a wonderful opportunity for the instructor to discuss the importance of wonder in work with children, as well as to model the importance of asking good questions in response to the students' questions (rather than just answering), such as "Why do you think that is?" and having them collaboratively investigate the answers.

Fostering Discussions about Nutrition, Food Equity, and Access

The hydroponic gardens can foster discussions of healthy food options, and the availability of fresh food for young children and their families. There are excellent resources that can support these discussions, such as the TED talk by Ron Finley, which talks about urban gardening and the lack of access to healthy fresh food in high-poverty areas. There is also the TED talk and the book, *The Green Machine*, by Stephen Ritz, a high school teacher in the South Bronx who uses hydroponics in the classroom with his students. These TED talks, in particular, are powerful for students as they help them to see the societal and educational potential of gardening, and fresh food as a social justice issue, especially in low-income urban environments.

Modeling Social-Emotional Teaching and Learning

The hydroponic gardens are a valuable way to incorporate social-emotional learning into the classroom. Competencies such as self-awareness, growth mindset, collaboration, and creating community in the classroom can be authentically fostered through the gardens. The sense of joy and pride that a child (and a preservice teacher!) feels when they successfully grow strawberries or tomatoes and share them with their peers is invaluable.

Part of the planning process of what to grow in the hydroponic gardens should include the goal for what is grown. This is a great way to model understanding by design curriculum planning—starting with the end goal and working from there. Goals can include the academic goals as well as social goals of creating community in the classroom. Cumulating activities can include a smoothie and salad party (or a "saladbration," as they do at Hopewell Elementary School), or a planned donation to a local food pantry.

In addition, at the elementary school the STEM facilitator creates maintenance forms with a checklist for children. Doing this with preservice teachers provides a sense of responsibility for the gardens and helps preservice teachers consider how they could create "jobs" for students in their future classrooms. Depending on what works best, sometimes the gardens may be housed in the room where the class meets. Having the gardens on wheels allows more flexibility to bring them in hallways or from room to room. If the gardens are kept in a separate place and not moveable the class can take a "field trip" to the room and use clipboards with their packets attached.

If possible, have students grow their own plants to foster a sense of responsibility for the plant. It can also lead to other benefits, such as discussing developing a growth mindset, especially if the plant doesn't grow. One semester, for some reason some seeds did not sprout in the classroom garden. Even though each student planted two each, a few students ended up not having a seed sprout (even with the extras planted by the instructor!). The other students volunteered to share their plant or to give their plant to their peer. These little acts of kindness in the face of adversity led to a wonderful discussion and a very teachable moment for the students.

Building Preservice Teachers' Connection to Nature

One of the most impactful aspects of using the hydroponic gardens with preservice teachers is developing their connection to nature. This is the first step for them to develop a connection in children. The joy felt when a pepper plant or lettuce actually grows, or the taste of an edible flower that they planted, is something that many college students have never experienced. Many of them feel removed and isolated from the natural world and gardening can help them connect or reconnect with nature.

One way to have them experience this connection is through having them grow their own plants in the garden. As part of the course, have them choose the seed, plant it, transfer it, and cull, harvest, and share it at the end of the semester. They can take pictures and create a notebook documenting their seed's growth (Padlet.com or WeVideo are great platforms for this). Many of the students spontaneously take selfies with their plants.

Another option is to give them a yogurt cup with an *Oasis* cube or other medium for them to grow at their plants at home and then share pictures in class of their plants. This opportunity to be responsible for their plants over the course of the semester is a powerful conduit for connecting to nature.

Hydroponics can be an impactful tool for teaching and learning, and provides an easy and accessible way to bring nature into the college and early childhood classrooms. However, indoor gardening should not replace outdoor-based learning. Going outside is beneficial for all people—children and adults. It is problematic that school learning has become almost exclusively an indoor endeavor. Instead, the gap between indoor and outdoor spaces should be fluid, a worn path in both directions.

As part of the course, it is essential to incorporate walks outside or have an assignment that requires student teachers to visit a park or somehow explore the natural world and consider the benefits for themselves and students. Even though the hydroponics can be indoors, it is a more impactful experience for students when connected to outdoor academic learning. For example, students can make comparisons of the same plant grown indoors and outside, consider the root systems (visible with hydroponics but not outside) as well as pollination, habitats, and ecosystems.

LESSONS LEARNED

Sometimes it can be difficult to take the risk and bring new things into the classroom, even as a college professor! One of the many benefits of the gardens is that the instructor can and should be open about their learning process and, if it is the case, that they are new to using the gardens as well. Having the students participate in all aspects of the gardens, including getting funding, figuring out how to set up and maintain the gardens, developing curriculum, and reflecting on how the instructor can improve the use of the gardens for future students is essential.

Some of the hardest aspects of using the gardens in a course that has to cover so many other things is finding the time for integrating the gardens in meaningful ways, and finding ways to use the gardens with larger classes of 25 students or more. These are similar problems that early childhood teachers face, so there are opportunities for reflection with the students about how the gardens could be better integrated into the coursework and avoid them feeling like an add-on.

It is not always possible to work with schools who use hydroponic gardens, and it isn't necessary; however, if it is possible, it is a powerful opportunity for students to observe teachers teaching with gardens. Their familiarity with the hydroponics from the college builds their confidence and knowledge for using them in the field. Students at The College of New Jersey have developed lessons using the gardens for units on pollination (second grade), Egypt (third grade), care and appreciation of the Earth (first grade), and living and nonliving things (kindergarten), to name a few. Upon graduation, numerous students have brought hydroponic gardens to their own classrooms and schools. This is perhaps the best evidence that using hydroponic gardens is an impactful practice for early childhood preservice teachers!

RECOMMENDED WEBSITES AND ORGANIZATIONS

Ron Finley TED Talk: *A Guerilla Gardener in South Central LA*
Stephen Ritz TED Talk and *The Green Bronx Machine* webpage
Tower Garden website
Hopewell Elementary Vertical Farming Initiative on Twitter: @HESVerticalFarm
National Farm to School Network
Natural Start Alliance
Children & Nature Network
Shelburne Farms

BIBLIOGRAPHY

Blank, R. K. (2012). *What is the impact of decline in science instructional time in elementary school?* Paper prepared for the Noyce Foundation. Retrieved from http://www.csss-science.org/downloads/NAEPElemScienceData.pdf

Cheng, J. C. H., & Monroe, M. C. (2010). Connection to nature: Children's affective attitude toward nature. *Environment and Behavior, 44*, 31–49.

Horizon Research, Inc. (2013). The 2012 national survey of science and mathematics education: Highlights report. Chapel Hill, NC.

Kellert, Stephen R. (2005). Nature and childhood development. In *Building for life: Designing and understanding the human-nature connection.* Washington, DC: Island Press.

McClure, E. R., Guernsey, L., Clements, D. H., Bales, S. N., Nichols, J., Kendall-Taylor, N., & Levine, M. H. (2017) *STEM starts early: Grounding science, technology, engineering, and math education in early childhood.* New York: The Joan Ganz Cooney Center at Sesame Workshop.

National Science Teachers Association (NSTA). (2018). *NSTA position statement: Elementary school science.* Arlington, VA: NSTA.

North American Association for Environmental Education (NAAEE). (2017a). *Stanford analysis reveals wide array of benefits from environmental education.* Washington, DC: NAAEE. Retrieved from https://cdn.naaee.org/sites/default/files/eeworks/files/k-12_student_key_findings.pdf

North American Association for Environmental Education (NAAEE). (2017b). *Nature preschools and forest kindergartens: 2017 national survey.* Washington, DC: NAAEE.

Ozer, Emily J. (2007). The effects of school gardens on students and schools: Conceptualization and considerations for maximizing healthy development. *Health Education & Behavior, 34*(6), 846–863. doi:10.1177/1090198106289002

Rahm, J. (2002). Emergent learning opportunities in an inner-city youth gardening program. *Journal of Research in Science Teaching, 39,* 164–184. doi:10.1002/tea.10015

Trent-Brown, S. A., Vanderveen, J. D., Cotter, R., Hawkins, K., Schab, A., & Dykstra, S. (2011). *Effects of a nature-based science enrichment program on preschool children's health, activity preferences, self-efficacy, and cognition.* Holland, MI: Outdoor Discovery Center, Macatawa Greenway.

Chapter Nine

Let's Have a Mathematical Conversation

Assessing Preservice Teachers' Ability to Do Mathematics

Alan Bates

Mathematics has always been a subject that makes students of all ages cringe. Preservice teachers are no exception. Many have had bad experiences with teachers because of timed tests, or they remember the many worksheets that were given to them when they were younger. As a result, they tend to have high anxiety around mathematical understanding and methodology (Brady & Bowd, 2005; Harper & Danne, 1998); also, they are more likely to indicate negative views such as "mathematics is my enemy" and "math is something I hate" when asked to express their views of mathematics (Cady & Rearden, 2007). They also tend to have low mathematics self-efficacy (Bates, Latham, & Kim, 2011), which refers to one's belief in their ability to do mathematics (Betz & Hackett, 1983).

The fact that preservice teachers have high math anxiety and lower mathematics self-efficacy is alarming considering their responsibility for teaching young children about mathematics and setting the foundation for future mathematics learning. It is vital that early childhood mathematics educators provide experiences within their courses that can increase preservice teachers' mathematics self-efficacy as well as their mathematics abilities. The impactful practice described in this chapter is an assessment used in an early childhood mathematics methods course that was designed to assess preservice teachers' understanding of, and ability to teach, mathematics as well as increase their confidence in teaching mathematics.

A DIFFERENT TYPE OF ASSESSMENT

With the Common Core State Standards for mathematics being used in many states and with its emphasis on conceptual understanding for students, it is important that preservice teachers have opportunities to learn and develop a conceptual understanding of mathematics concepts. This requires preservice teachers to be exposed to a wide variety of experiences. The assessment described in this chapter is one unique and effective way of allowing students to practice and demonstrate their mathematical knowledge. The assessment came about through both the instructor's and preservice teachers' frustration with a traditional paper and pencil test.

The course in which this assessment was implemented, "Teaching Early Childhood Mathematics," is taken by students during the second semester of their junior year. The prerequisites include at least one general education mathematics course, which is their first and only mathematics methods course. The instructor taught this course for several years and initially used traditional written quizzes and exams.

The instructor became increasingly frustrated with the lack of clarity provided in the students' responses and believed their true understanding was not adequately represented. In the course, students learn new methods of doing mathematics, specifically regarding computation and working with fractions, and thus must learn both how to perform and introduce the methods. The focus of the course and embedded assessments was to have students demonstrate a conceptual understanding of these various mathematical concepts.

Semester after semester, students complained about the quizzes and the final. They expressed that writing it all down on paper was more difficult than verbally explaining it. Typical responses from students include, "I know how to do it but it takes too long to write it all down," and "Isn't there a better way to show you that I know how to do it?" So one semester, the instructor decided to offer an oral, one-on-one final for interested students. Students would demonstrate their knowledge verbally instead of using the traditional paper and pencil format. This was offered for two consecutive semesters and nobody took the opportunity.

The instructor realized that unless it was a requirement, students would not choose an oral final. The format was seen as intimidating; students needed to be more familiar with the material to answer questions right on the spot. They have very little time to think through the problem and have no chance to attempt alternate ways to check their answers. The instructor decided to require students to take the oral final in place of the traditional pencil and paper final. However, quizzes were still administered in the traditional paper and pencil format. Students were provided practice solving problems in a traditional assessment format.

This assessment is impactful in many ways. Students have a more authentic experience compared to a written exam and walk away with specific practice in explaining algorithms and fraction concepts, possibly giving them more confidence in their computational skills. Students do more than just answer mathematics problems with paper and pencil; they teach as if they were teaching a student, paying close attention to the use of academic language and the materials they use. Trying to break students' habit of using terms such as "borrow" and "carry" and replacing them with the terms such as "regroup" and "trade" is a key goal of the class, as it is important that preservice teachers are using the proper language of the discipline.

Many of the students do not have the opportunity to teach various math concepts in their clinical experiences. Moreover, these ways of solving and thinking about problems are new to many of the students, so to be able to do it face-to-face and verbally, provides them with an opportunity to practice teaching these concepts. They receive immediate feedback as they are "teaching" the concepts and can make adjustments as needed. There is no "guessing" or leaving questions blank as might happen on a paper and pencil exam. The instructor offers prompts and encouragement until something "clicks" within a student. For example, the instructor may remind them of a related class activity or ask a question such as, "What does a child do when they 'borrow'?"

The face-to-face exam also encourages students to study more. They want to ensure they are prepared when they meet with the instructor one-on-one. Students spend more time working with each other outside of class and attending the instructor's office hours. Students borrow materials such as base ten blocks and fraction cubes from the instructor so they can practice at home and in their groups. So ultimately, the more significant impact is on the students' learning of the material as well as their desire to truly understand the content.

IMPLEMENTATION

Implementing this assessment is both challenging and time consuming for many reasons. Students are very hesitant and nervous about the prospect of meeting with the instructor one-on-one and being asked questions on the spot. They are notified about the format of the final at the beginning of the semester and reminded about it throughout the semester and especially during class activities that are designed to prepare them for the oral, one-on-one final (see textbox 9.1).

> ### TEXTBOX 9.1. FINAL EXAM GUIDELINES
>
> A final exam will be given during final examinations week and will include both an online and oral, one-on-one portion. The online portion will be open during finals week and can be taken any time by the student. It will focus on early childhood mathematics concept definitions and application. The one-on-one portion of the exam will focus on computation (addition, subtraction, multiplication, and division) and fractions with an emphasis on demonstrating a conceptual understanding. It is intended to be a mathematical conversation and opportunity to really explore your understanding of the concepts. The one-on-one exam will not be held during the university assigned time; instead, students will be asked to sign up online for an appropriate time based on their availability for the one-on-one portion of the exam. Students will be able to work around their other course final. The final exam is required of all students.

The final should not be introduced as an exam, but instead as a mathematical conversation. This helps lighten the impact on students but also stresses the point that it is not a traditional final; it is intended to be a give and take between the instructor and student. It is not only used as an assessment but also as one last opportunity for students to ask questions, receive feedback, and clarify their understanding of various concepts with which they may be struggling. Students are told and reminded throughout the semester that they will be prepared when the time comes if they participate in class and study for quizzes. They also like to hear that past students have been successful with the format.

Considerations Prior to Implementation

About halfway through the semester, the instructor notifies the class about signing up for the final. Identifying a sufficient amount of time can be challenging. Instead of using the university assigned final period, which is typically less than the needed time, various times should be made available during the last week of the semester and finals week, as the instructor's schedule allows.

The length of the final varies depending on how many questions the instructor asks and how much prompting and feedback is needed. An hour per student is sufficient for the final, with some students finishing earlier than others. Typically, well-prepared students take less time than those students who are less prepared. Also, additional time may be needed for more nervous students, as the instructor may have to calm their nerves before beginning the assessment.

The time commitment needed is a challenge for implementing this type of exam. With a range of 20 to 30 students enrolled in the course, it can take up to 15 to 30 hours of the instructor's time; but that is not inconsistent with the time it would take to grade final projects or paper and pencil final exams. Questions are prepared ahead of time and an effort is made to consider student's individual struggles throughout the semester based on their performance on previous quizzes and assignments. For example, if a student struggled with subtraction computation more so than addition, their questions might focus more heavily on subtraction.

The website signupgenius.com or a similar system could be used to manage the schedule and provide easy access for the students. Signupgenius.com enables students to sign up for times and change times if necessary outside of class, and it allows easy access to the schedule online. Students could also email each other directly to exchange any scheduled times. The system notifies the instructor if changes are made. Finding space for giving the exam is also a challenge, typically a conference room with a whiteboard and table is used since the students will need it to demonstrate the concepts. Many whiteboard markers will also be required!

Additionally, it is important to provide study sessions if time allows and to highly suggest to the students that they practice with their roommates or parents. Students find it helpful to explain these new strategies and algorithms to people who do not really know them. They find it especially rewarding and it serves two purposes: helping them practice and showing their parents what they are learning in the class. Even college students want to impress their parents!

To make the most out of the exam for the students, the instructor must maintain accurate records of how students perform on previous quizzes and in-class assignments. In addition to the type of problems missed, the instructor records the numbers involved and the strategy or algorithm used. For example, if a student struggles with her seven multiplication facts, the instructor includes those within the computation problems. Or if a student struggles with a nontraditional algorithm, the instructor includes that algorithm in the final.

It is not possible to include questions for all the concepts due to the limited time with the student and needing sufficient time to ask questions and prompt or discuss if required. The goal is to target the exam to each student's needs. Students are asked anywhere between 10 to 15 questions, which varies based on their responses and the assistance needed by the students during the exam. As they provide their answers, the instructor asks questions from a child's perspective as well as questions that provide an opportunity for the student to demonstrate a more in-depth knowledge of the concepts. To ensure that a variety of questions are asked, questions are grouped by topic areas (see textbox 9.2).

> ## TEXTBOX 9.2. FINAL EXAM TOPICS
>
> 1. **Invented Strategies**
>   Term used by Van de Walle, Lovin, Karp, and Bay-Williams (2018) to describe non-algorithm strategies to solve problems; these are based on children understanding and using their base ten knowledge.
>   Students should be able to solve these problems in different ways and to explain how they solve them and explain them as they would to young children.
>
>   - Addition
>   - Subtraction
>   - Multiplication
>   - Division
>
> 2. **Algorithms**
>   Traditional, left-to-right, and other algorithms as discussed in class—where appropriate, students should know how to explain each using base ten models. Think in terms of how one would introduce them to young children.
>
> 3. **Fractions**
>   Students should be able to demonstrate an understanding of the following:
>
>   - Fractions using a number line
>   - Conceptual thought patterns for comparing fractions (not relying on algorithms but instead using one-half, and the whole as a reference and considering the size and quantity of the parts of the fractions)
>   - Equivalent fractions

Successful Implementation

Prior to beginning each exam, the instructor asks if the student has any questions to allow for any last-minute clarifications. The instructor allows students to choose which topic area to begin from. The student then selects an area they are most comfortable with, thus easing them into the testing format.

The instructor asks students to introduce specific algorithms as if they were introducing them to children and then the instructor poses questions as a child might throughout the students' explanations. The instructor may also ask students to use non-algorithm strategies to solve problems, either on their own or to present them in a way they would with children. Materials such as counters, Unifix cubes, fraction circles, and so forth, are provided for students to use as part of their response. The use of materials may not be optional, but this is at the instructor's discretion.

Students use base ten blocks in both solving problems and their introduction of algorithms, since a primary focus of the course is for students to gain a conceptual understanding of computational algorithms. The instructor takes advantage of learning opportunities that present themselves throughout the interaction. For example, if the instructor notices the student using the same types of strategies in solving problems, alternate ways may be suggested or explained.

Additional questions require the instructor to solve a problem in front of the student to see if the student can gauge the "child's" understanding and identify strategies used. The instructor solves various problems and the student will have to recognize errors and make decisions on how to move the child forward. The goal is to get students to pose questions to the instructor (as the child) rather than just correcting the child.

For every question, it is essential that the instructor listens for the appropriate mathematical language in the students' responses and not just for the correct answer. Students will often have the steps down but use incorrect language. The instructor offers prompts that allow the students to correct themselves. Providing these prompts at the end of the explanation is most effective as some students will lose their train of thought. A statement such as, "Your explanation was right on target, however, you used some nonmathematical terminology. Please start over, focusing specifically on the correct terminology," lets the students know they were on the right track but needed the correct language.

Assessing Students

One other aspect to consider in implementing this type of exam is how to assess the student's performance on the assessment. Just as the assessment itself may vary based on the student's need, the grading will vary as well. As the student answers each question, points are deducted if a student asks questions, requires prompting, or initially provides incorrect responses.

A perfect score on the exam occurs when a student answers each question thoroughly and correctly, uses materials when appropriate, and requires no prompting. A 1/2 to 1 point deduction is made for mistakes or prompts needed on each of the questions, depending on the type of mistake or prompt that is required. Simple basic fact errors result in -1/2 point, while using incorrect strategies or terminology results in -1 point. If students need a full prompt to begin a problem, they will have a point reduced.

A rubric has never been used to assess the final since each final looks very different depending on students' needs. The point deduction system has worked the best and is clearly explained to the students beforehand. The goal of the instructor is to identify students' understanding rather than focus on counting points for the grade. Students should not be worried about their grade but focus on this last opportunity to demonstrate what they know and learn what they don't know. Results of the final are discussed with students immediately and point deductions are clearly explained. Any student concerns can be addressed at that point.

Sample Questions

Below are sample questions, listed in the categories described above, which have been used by the instructor on previous exams. Some numbers are included while others are left blank as indicated by the number sign. This allows the instructor to substitute numbers on the spot so the numbers can be varied for each student. Also, some of the problems mention multiple strategies, algorithms, and so forth, but the instructor decides what to assess in each of the questions.

Invented Strategies—The questions in this category allow students to demonstrate their ability to either solve the problems presented on their own or explain the strategies as if they were working with a child. Another variation of these type of problems is for the instructor to solve the problems in front of the student and ask the student to identify what strategy is being used and what mistakes, if any, were made. Also, for any of these questions, the instructor can ask the student a "why" question during the solving of the problem, such as, "Why did you take apart 47 into 4 tens and 7 ones?" or "Where did you get those 7 ones from?"

1. Using the problem 447 ÷ 7 (sample), walk me through the missing factor strategy as if I were a child who did not understand it.
2. Using the problem, ## - ## and # + #, walk me through two subtraction invented strategies, one take away and one counting up, and two addition invented strategies, as if I were a child who did not understand them.
3. Using the problem, ## x #, walk me through two multiplication invented strategies as if I were a child who did not understand them.

Algorithms—The questions listed below focus on algorithms for each of the operations. Many students are familiar with the traditional algorithms although they may have difficulty explaining them or they may use incorrect language when describing the steps of the problem. A key goal of this section is having students focus on the use of appropriate mathematical language. Students will commonly use terms such as "borrow," "cancel," and "goes into," instead of terms such as "trade," "regroup," and "equal groups."

1. Solve and explain the problem 81 - 46, using both right-to-left and left-to-right subtraction algorithms. Use base ten blocks along with your explanation.
2. Explain and demonstrate how you would solve ## x ## [or # x ##] using the left-to-right method, traditional right-to-left method, and/or the lattice method of multiplication.
3. Show how you would introduce the column division algorithm (or the traditional long division algorithm) with base ten blocks. You can assume that the child knows how to solve a division problem using the blocks but has no knowledge of the column or long division algorithm. Use the problem 541 ÷ 4. [Here, it is important for students to connect the steps of the algorithm to the corresponding use of the base ten blocks. Paper plates can be provided to assist students in showing the number of groups and allowing a clearer distinction of where the blocks should be placed.]
4. Solve and explain the problem ## + ##, using the traditional (right-to-left) algorithm, the left-to-right algorithm, and/or column addition. Use base ten blocks along with your explanation.
5. Student error analysis: 635 + 58. Be prepared to identify and explain the error that I make to me as if I were a student. You will also have to provide me a strategy that I could use to prevent the same error in the future. You may use base ten blocks in your explanation. [This is an example of a problem where the instructor makes common mistakes such as forgetting to trade or regroup or simple basic fact mistakes. The strategy can be used with any of the operations, although it is typically used more with addition and subtraction.]

Fractions—The goal of the fraction section is to allow students to demonstrate a conceptual understanding of fractions. Many preservice students have only a procedural understanding of comparing or converting fractions into mixed or improper fractions. Students are allowed and encouraged to use graph paper, number lines, fraction circles, and fraction cubes during their explanations. If they use any of those items, the instructor says something such as, "I don't understand what you just said, how might you show me what you just explained?" Students are asked to use more than one of the resources to assure they understand each of them. Typically, number lines provide the highest level of challenge for the students.

1. Using your choice of materials and the conceptual thought patterns of comparison, explain which fraction is greater in each of these problems:

    a. 3/8 or 4/6
    b. 9/10 or 7/8

2. Explain conceptually why the two fractions 1/3 and 3/9 are considered equivalent fractions.
3. Explain conceptually how to convert 3 1/4 to an improper fraction.
4. Explain conceptually why 13/3 is equal to 4 1/3.
5. Explain conceptually why the two fractions 1/2 and 4/8 are considered equivalent fractions.

LESSONS LEARNED

Although students are hesitant, nervous, or even outright frightened about the one-on-one oral exam, every student has come away from the experience stating that they preferred it over a traditional paper and pencil exam. Students comment that it is easier to demonstrate what they know about the concepts and appreciate the fact they can learn as they go since they are able to ask questions of the instructor during the assessment.

The main goal of the exam is to assess students' learning over the semester, but it is also the last opportunity the instructor has to clarify students' understanding, demonstrate concepts, and so forth. Unlike a paper and pencil test, it allows further questioning, which can ultimately provide a better picture of students' understanding. Overall, students are more likely to walk away with a better understanding of the various concepts assessed.

Students have overwhelmingly said they would recommend keeping the oral final in the course and that they feel they learned much more in their preparation for this exam compared to traditional exams. They admit that the preparation and process are stressful but overall the experience is worth it. Students walk away from the experience with appreciation that it is very much a "give and take" between the instructor and student.

The instructor has learned a great deal from implementing this type of exam because it has positively impacted students' understanding of course material. The instructor gained a better sense of the types of understanding the students have. What students demonstrate on a paper exam is much different than when standing in front of the instructor. The level of competency for each student becomes more evident, especially for basic fact knowledge.

When face-to-face, it is much easier to know whether students truly are fluent with their basic facts, such as their times tables, simple addition facts, and so forth. On a paper and pencil test, they can take their time and use other strategies to solve a problem, so the instructor may assume fluency but would never know. Because of this, providing the required practice of basic fact skills is essential as well. More time is now given in class for students to play basic fact games where previously they had been only briefly introduced as good options for children and not as practice opportunities for university students.

Results from initial implementation have influenced how the instructor teaches the mathematical concepts and the type of practice and assignments that are provided. Instructors must provide many examples and practice during class time. Pairing the students to practice and encouraging them to talk through explanations has been important. Also, having students go up in front of the class to practice problems has become a more frequent practice than in the past.

The instructor has learned that preparing the students mentally for the exam is very important. Putting their minds at ease is a necessity and begins the first week of the semester when the idea is first introduced. Emphasis is not on the oral, one-on-one aspect but more so on the fact that it is focused on their learning and that it is easier to explain verbally than it is to write. Stressing that it is more of a conversation than a traditional assessment is meant to create a relaxed context. Students are told that they will have a chance to ask questions and receive clarification throughout the exam.

Since beginning the implementation of this type of exam, the instructor has made a few mistakes along the way. The first few times the final was offered, the instructor included the assessment of noncomputational items such as creating story problems, basic fact strategies, and early mathematics concepts such as counting principles, one-to-one correspondence, subitizing, and so forth. These concepts do not lend themselves well to a face-to-face format.

The instructor realized that giving more time for the exam is imperative for the learning process. At first, only 30 minutes were given and it was not enough time to allow for any discussion. Depending on the number of students in a section, this could be a tiring process for the instructor. Time must be allowed for instructor breaks between students and the instructor needs sufficient time to plan for each student. It is more impactful for students when the exam is modified based on their needs. Without this process, students may get questions that they have already mastered and not get questions they need more practice with.

When first implementing this final, the instructor provided a list of times to students and had them sign up in class; but after having students forget their times, emailing at the last minute, or not showing up, the decision was made to use www.signupgenius.com, described above. Another challenge the instructor faced was that of extremely nervous or unprepared students. Initially, the instructor was not prepared for students physically shaking or being on the verge of tears. Time must be taken to make them feel as relaxed as possible.

On rare occasions, students come to the final unprepared. These students demonstrate little knowledge right out of the gate and may even cry when they hear the first question. They realize immediately that they are not prepared. After a few instances, the instructor learned to stop the exam right away and suggest the student reschedule for a later time and use the time to practice. This has been beneficial for the instructor and student the couple of times it was done.

Another issue is since the test is spread out over a few days, there is always the chance that questions are shared. The first two semesters the instructor used the same questions and numbers for each student, but once the instructor realized that students were sharing that information, it was necessary to at least change the numbers used in the various problems. This evolved into a more custom fit exam, and students are notified of this from the beginning. Once the instructor began varying the tests to meet individual needs, it has not been an issue.

In summary, this chapter has introduced a unique way of assessing students in an early childhood mathematics course. Implementing an oral, one-on-one final allows students to demonstrate their true understanding of various math concepts and can enable them to develop an impactful practice "teaching" those concepts. The instructor has an opportunity to authentically assess the students' understanding and teaching abilities with the added opportunity to prompt and ask appropriate questions. Although the experience can be both stressful and time consuming, it is well worth the effort for both student and instructor. Hopefully this results in the students having a conceptual understanding and being more comfortable with teaching various concepts.

RECOMMENDED RESOURCES

Ashlock, Robert B. (2010). *Error patterns in computation: Using error patterns to help each student learn* (10th ed.). Boston: Allyn & Bacon.

Carpenter, Thomas P., Fennema, Elizabeth, Loef Franke, Megan, Levi, Linda, & Empson, Susan B. (2015). *Children's mathematics: Cognitively guided instruction* (2nd ed.). Portsmouth, NH: Heinemann.

Empson, Susan B., & Levi, Linda. (2011). *Extending children's mathematics: Fractions and decimals*. Portsmouth, NH: Heinemann.

Parrish, Sherry. (2014). *Number talks: Helping children build mental math and computation strategies*. Sausalito, CA: Math Solutions.
Parrish, Sherry, & Dominick, Ann. (2016). *Number talks: Fractions, decimals, and percentages*. Sausalito, CA: Math Solutions.
Spangler, David B. (2010). *Strategies for teaching whole number computation: Using error analysis for intervention and assessment*. Thousand Oaks, CA: Corwin.
Van de Walle, John A., Lovin, LouAnn H., Karp, Karen S., & Bay-Williams, Jennifer M. (2018). *Teaching student-centered mathematics: Grades pre-k-2* (vol. 1, 3rd ed.). Boston: Allyn & Bacon.
University of Chicago. (n.d.). Everyday mathematics. Resource and Information Center. Retrieved from http://everydaymath.uchicago.edu/teaching-topics/computation/
Utah State University. (n.d.). National Library of Virtual Manipulatives. Retrieved from http://nlvm.usu.edu/en/nav/vlibrary.html

BIBLIOGRAPHY

Bates, Alan, Latham, Nancy, & Kim, Jin-ah. (2011). Linking preservice teachers' mathematics teaching efficacy to their mathematical performance. *School Science Mathematics*, *111*(7), 325–333.
Betz, Nancy, & Hackett, Gail. (1983). The relationship of mathematics self-efficacy expectations to the selection of science-based college majors. *Journal of Vocational Behavior*, *23*, 329–345.
Brady, Patrick, & Bowd, Alan. (2005). Mathematics anxiety, prior experience and confidence to teach mathematics among pre-service education students. *Teachers and Teaching: Theory and Practice*, *11*, 37–46.
Cady, Jo Ann, & Rearden, Kristin. (2007). Pre-service teachers beliefs about knowledge, mathematics, and science. *School Science and Mathematics*, *107*(6), 236–245.
Harper, Norma, & Daane, C. J. (1998). Causes and reductions of math anxiety in pre-service elementary teachers. *Action in Teacher Education*, *19*, 29–38.
Van de Walle, John, Lovin, LouAnn H., Karp, Karen, & Bay-Williams, Jennifer M. (2018). *Teaching student-centered mathematics: Developmentally appropriate instruction for grades prek-2*. New York: Pearson.

Chapter Ten

Connecting Things in ECE Teaching and Learning

The "Six Objects Task"

Alyse C. Hachey

This chapter describes a teaching activity, the "Six Objects Task," that can be utilized during early childhood education (ECE) teacher preparation or continuing educational development, particularly courses devoted to curriculum generally or early play-based teaching methods and art education specifically. In the "Six Objects Task," participants use six everyday objects in a series of interesting and engaging problems that require hands-on, play-based, multimodal participation. Therefore, regardless of the purpose of its use (of which there are many), just as a learning activity alone, it models impactful practice in ECE.

In many hands-on, play-based learning situations, preservice and in-service teachers are asked to pretend they are children as they engage in an activity. While these experiences do provide valuable examples, they typically are not mentally challenging at an adult level. The "Six Objects Task" is unique in that although it is developmentally appropriate to use the activity with children aged four to eight, it also, when done by adults, is flexible enough to allow for sophisticated adult thinking. Because of this, teachers can apply their own adult meaning to the experience, rather than feeling a sense of mental disconnect while assuming the role of a child. This has a three-fold benefit: Teachers tend to be genuinely engrossed and motivated *during* the activity, they tend to implicitly connect a learning experience with fun and play, and they walk away with an activity that can also be immediately used, in whole or part, in their early childhood classrooms.

Additionally, the "Six Objects Task" is impactful in terms of its versatility. This activity applies to not only many ECE topics but also to various teacher preparation courses and professional development situations. Some examples of its usefulness have been demonstrated through teacher training at all levels (e.g., in preservice preparation play theory class and during in-service training in STEAM education; in masters-level ECE pedagogy courses). Also, it has been successfully implemented with groups from as little as 10 to as large as 80 participants. Moreover, there is minimal setup and only a few materials required for the instructor to pull it off. Finally, the activity is versatile in the time it takes to do, easily shortened or modified by eliminating or merging steps to account for time limitations.

IMPLEMENTATION

The "Six Objects Task" is relatively easy to implement. The two steps are setting the stage and conducting the activity.

Setting the Stage

Prior to conducting the "Six Objects Task," the instructor should complete the following steps:

- Ask participants to bring any common six objects that are readily and cheaply available to them.
- Verbally provide some examples of objects, such as six paper clips, six leaves, six coffee stirrers, or six plastic forks, with the caveats that they 1) are all the same thing; 2) are all the same shape and size (relatively the same size if a natural object like a leaf or rock); 3) are not food or alive; and 4) do not need to be saved/used again.
- Tell participants that color does not matter (e.g., different colored paper clips are fine if they are all the same shape and size).

If the participants bring their own objects, have on hand several additional object sets (in case someone forgets objects).

Alternatively, a selection of sets of objects can be provided to participants. However, for best results, it is recommended to have at least eight different types of objects to choose from (a different set of objects for each participant or only a few duplicates is optimal, but from past experience, the minimum of eight types of objects will still ensure interesting results regardless of the group size). Further, because the core of this activity is based on personal choice and creativity, it is recommended that participants choose what objects they work with from the selection provided (rather than objects being assigned).

Connecting Things in ECE Teaching and Learning   113

The other supplies needed for the activity are "connectors." Connectors are 1) masking tape, 2) play-doh, and 3) yarn and scissors. The exact amount of each connector needed depends on the group size. For example, with 32 participants, it would be recommended to set up three different "connector stations" in different areas of the room; *each* connector station with a one-pound tub of play-doh, three rolls of masking tape, a ball of yarn, and three pairs of scissors. (Note: There is no set amount of each connector; the goal is to have enough of each connector available for everyone to use while sharing.)

The "Six Objects Task" works best if participants are sitting together at tables/pushed together desks; the exact number of people does not necessarily matter but if possible, try to ensure equal, even numbers per table/desk grouping. Also, ensure that the tables/desks are arranged so that participants can stand and walk an outer circle around the tables/desks. Finally, it is recommended to have the participants put all other objects (purses, folders, etc.) under the tables/desks, so all that is in front of them is their six objects intended for use during the activity.

Conducting the Activity

This section outlines the directions and experience-based suggestions for the instructor as they implement the design challenge.

Experiencing Simple Open-Ended Designing and Redesigning

1. *Let's Design.* Invite the participants to start: "I would like you to create a design so that all of your six objects touch in some way. Keep working with your objects until you have a design that you are happy with."

   (Past experience suggests adults can be unsure in open-ended situations, so they may ask for clarification or an example or seem initially confused. Just keep repeating the directions; do not explicitly provide a design example. Remind participants that any design is fine if *they* are happy with it, as long as all the objects touch. This first design task takes about one to two minutes. There is likely to be little talking between participants, and most designs will be 2-D.)

2. *Rearrange and Repeat.* Invite the participants to take one last look at their initial design, then ask them to separate their objects. Provide the next invitation: "I would like you to again create a design so that all of your six objects touch in some way. Please make a *different* design than the one you just made. Keep working with your objects until you have a new design you are happy with. When you are happy with your design, please stand up behind your chair." Once everyone is standing,

invite the group to form an outer circle around the tables/desks. Provide the directions: "Let's walk all the way around once, all going left, and look at each other's designs. Let's look this time with eyes on and hands off . . . no touching please."

(Past experience suggests the new design will again take about one minute to make. There likely will be little talking and most designs will remain 2-D. Even though the directions only referred to no touching, likely people will also not be talking as they circle and look at the designs.)

3. *Design while Challenging Group Norms.* Once everyone is sitting again, ask them to separate their objects if they have not already done so. Then provide the next invitation: "I would like you to create a design again so that all of your six objects touch in some way. Please make a completely different design from both of your previous designs. Keep working with your objects until you have a new design you are happy with. When you are happy with your design, please stand up." Before circling, provide the directions: "Let's all walk around once and look at each other's designs. Let's walk this time, with eyes on and *hands-on*, too. This means as you look at a design, if you can see or imagine another design using those objects, you are welcome to *go and change* the objects to the design you imagine. You can change any design you see as we walk around, whether it is yours or another person's design."

When participants get back *close* to their chair, invite them to look at the design their objects are now in: "Before you sit, take a look at your objects. Are they in the same design you left them in? Are they in a design you had previously? Is it a design you thought of but did not use or are they in a design that you did not even think of? Once you have looked at how your design is now, you can take a seat." (Note: These are just meant as hypothetical questions so participants examine what they find before immediately sitting and separating their objects; people may or may not call out answers.)

(Past experience suggests the latest design will again mostly be 2-D, take about one minute to complete, and people will just fall in and start circling. Because adults usually have been culturally trained not to touch other people's work, participants may not initially jump out of the circle to go and change up designs [even though they are directly invited to do so, adults pretty much never spontaneously touch other's designs]. If the participants circle about a quarter of the way around and no designs have been changed, then go and start changing up designs and continue doing so until other participants join in. Remind participants that it is an "eyes-on and hands-on" time. With a little added encouragement, one or two participants will usually start changing up designs, and then others will freely join in.)

Experiencing Complex and Collaborative Open-Ended Designing and Redesigning

1. *Let's connect.* Ask participants to separate their objects (if needed). Provide the fourth invitation: "Now, I am going to change things up a bit. I would still like you to create a design so that all six of your objects touch in some way. However, this time, you are required to use a connector. What is a connector? A connector is masking tape, play-doh, or yarn. (Hold up an example of each when named.) You can use any connector or any combination of connector. So, you could join your objects to form your design using tape, or play-doh, or yarn. Or you could use tape and play-doh, or tape and yarn, or play-doh and yarn. Or, you could even use all three connectors if you want! Pick the connector or combination of connectors that you think will work best for your latest design. You need to still be sure all of your six objects touch and that you use at least one of the connectors provided. As before, keep working with your objects and connectors until you have a new design you are happy with. When you are happy with your design, please stand up." (Provide some additional directions as to where participants can access the connector supplies.) Once everyone is standing behind their chairs, repeat the circling and viewing exercise just the same as task 2—"eyes on and hands off . . . no touching please."

   (Past experience suggests this design task will generally take around five minutes. Many of the designs will now be 3-D and will resemble common objects [i.e., caterpillars, houses, flowers, etc.]. People who get finished with their design early can be asked to take another look at their design and see if there is anything they want to change or add while they wait [this will often produce additional embellishment/decoration using connectors]. In comparison to the previous tasks, people will likely talk [as they negotiate getting connectors and look at/discuss how others use them]; similarly, there is often more talk when walking the circle and viewing designs [i.e., comments like "Oh, that is so cute!" and "Look, it's a caterpillar!"].)

2. *Design with a Friend.* As people start sitting again, go around the room and pair participants sitting next to each other by gesturing and repeating: "You two are now friends." Continue making pairs until everyone has a friend (with a team of three friends at the end if needed).

Provide the next invitation: "Before you separate your objects, please listen. You have six objects. And you now have a friend who has six objects. So now I would like you and your friend to create a single design so that *all 12* objects touch to form a single, joint design. You also still need to use at least one connector, or you can use any combination of connectors, to create your joint design. You can take your current designs apart and start from 12 separate objects, or you can start by using or modifying the two designs you currently have in some way; this choice is up to you and your friend. When you *and* your friend are happy with your joint design, please stand up." Then, repeat the circling and viewing exercise from tasks 2 and 4—"eyes on and hands off . . . no touching please."

(Past experience suggests this design task will generally take around eight minutes. As "friends" work together, everyone will be talking and socially interacting; laughing, exclamations of delight, or sorrow and signs of negotiation and group dynamics [leaders/followers] become apparent. Nearly all designs will be 3-D, have additional embellishment [e.g., play-doh will not only connect but have eyes], and be more easily recognizable as collections of objects interacting [i.e., a caterpillar on a bed of flowers]; participants will spontaneously label parts of designs during construction and while circling after. Physics often now come into play [gravity becomes an issue for designs and experimentation naturally occurs, as well as more discussion regarding the pros/cons of each connector and the actual usage/application of connectors to ensure stability]. Pairs who get finished early can be asked to take another look and to see if there is any last thing they want to change or add.)

3. *The More the Merrier.* The last invitation(s) consist of repeating task 5 several times while doubling up participants to form larger teams of "friends" with each repeat. For example, with 32 participants, pairs could be combined to form teams of 4 friends each and then repeat design task 5 using all of their 24 available objects. Then, the teams can double up again to form 4 teams of 8 participants, repeating task 5 using their 48 objects, and finally, participants can be combined into 2 teams of 16 each (or you can even add a final mega-design including all 32 participants).

The number of repeats depends on the total group size and time constraints (some of the middle doubling ups can be skipped if time is short). However, for participants to get the full experience of adding physical and social complexity, it is recommended that enough combining of participants and repeated designing happens until task 5 is experienced at least two times (three times total) and ends with at least two final large teams of "friends." Upon the last task 5 conducted, provide a final invitation: "This will be our last design. Once you and your final team of friends are happy with your design, please give your final masterpiece a title/name." As the final circling occurs, invite each team to share the name of their final design. As participants are sitting for the very last time, provide this final request: "Please, everyone, eyes on me. How long have we been doing this whole activity? No cheating by looking at the clock or your phone. How long in total have we been working with our objects to make designs?"

(Past experience suggests expressions of pride and enjoyment by teams will usually occur in the final circling. Before the debriefing, participants will often want to take pictures of their designs with their final team members. Clean-up of designs can happen before or after debriefing [depending on the focus, it is sometimes better to leave the designs up as a point of reference]. The final question asking participants about the time the activity took *always* produces incorrect answers; consistently participants mistake the length of engagement by shortening it by about half. This can be a great jumping off point for a discussion about why this long activity felt short [e.g., because participants were both physically and mentally involved, leading to deep engagement].)

Note: Another question that will produce an inaccurate answer is to ask during the debriefing if the activity had rules. Participants always quickly answer no, yet the activity is actually heavily regulated and full of rules. This can be a great jumping off point for discussions about why an activity full of rules does not feel like it has any (e.g., because it is open-ended and has opportunities for choice also embedded in it).

DEBRIEFING THE "SIX OBJECTS TASK"

On the surface, the "Six Objects Task" is an activity composed of simply connecting things. Yet, upon closer examination, it is a multifaceted example of play, of creative and divergent thinking, of construction, of collaboration, and ultimately, of ways to organize simple and complex open-ended learning experiences. The repeating design process, the changes in participant behaviors, and the design products that emerge during and across each of the tasks can serve as the basis for participants to explore their own and other's thinking. Thus, this activity serves as a rich experience that can be used as the focus of discussion on a multitude of ECE teaching and learning concepts, including making connections at the child and teacher level, play-based teaching practice, fostering creativity, and ECE STEM/STEAM education.

Making Connections

Often, good early childhood education, for both teachers and students, is truly the art of just connecting things. Every day, young children connect their prior knowledge with new experiences and events in their lives to expand what they know and how they will interact with the world moving forward. Thus, the "Six Objects Task" can serve as a metaphor for how children are connectors and constructors of knowledge/learning. This activity purposefully includes opportunities for discovery and repeated practice, which are two key components of how children acquire knowledge and develop skills. Further, this activity can be the starting point for instruction on the tenets of situated cognition—which contends that thinking processes are *situated* in the social and environmental context and hence, "are integral to agents-in-their-context-acting-for-a-purpose-and-with-tools" (Roth & Jornet, 2013, p. 473).

Every day in their professional lives teachers encounter separate "objects" (e.g., differential student needs, various learning/developmental aims, available materials, administrator input, parent/community influences, schedules, etc.) which they somehow have to connect into a cohesive curriculum design that meets everyone's needs, and often multiple goals. So, in this sense, teaching itself could be viewed as an iterative design task. From this lens, the "Six Objects Task," along with the design thinking model (see Recommended Resources) provides both a metaphor and a new, step-by-step concept for teachers to use to *design* curriculum (using prompts such as, "How is curriculum building like a design problem? What effect can collaboration and sharing of ideas have on curriculum design?"). Discussing the work of the ECE teacher from this perspective can serve to resituate and empower preservice and in-service ECE teachers as knowledge constructors themselves.

It can also be used as the starting point for instruction on major ECE or general learning theorists. For example, progressive theorists (such as Dewey, Pestalozzi, and Frobel) aver that children learn through direct manipulation and experience of objects, through which they can discover, arrange, invent, and control (see review in Marsh et al., 2017). Alternatively, Jean Piaget's assimilation and accommodation as the bases of knowledge construction through physical interactions and experiences can be demonstrated. A nature connection occurs with Vygotsky's (1978) notion of the sociocultural construction of knowledge, in which cognitive development stems from social interactions bound by culture. This activity is even relatable to critical theories, such as Paulo Freire's idea of "culturally meaningful curriculum construction" (Blikstein, 2013; Marsh et al., 2017) or the "Funds of Knowledge" (González, Moll, & Amanti, 2005), whereby authentically meaningful activities lead to thinking and solutions that can educate and empower the learner.

Play-Based Teaching Practice

Play-based teaching includes process-based versus product-based curriculum development; didactic versus child-centered teaching methods; balancing classroom management (rules) with student agency (choice), the impact of open-ended versus closed-ended materials, and the effect of instructional design on both children's social interaction and depth of thinking. Whether for young children or adults, a learning experience is impactful when it engages peoples' interests and senses, and when it opens up their minds to new ideas at the same time it allows them the freedom to make personal connections and construct meaning. If the goal is to expand perspective or in-service teachers' knowledge on play or child-centered curriculum or the need/benefit of open-ended, meaningful learning experiences in ECE, then that is the exact sort of experience that the teachers need to have themselves while learning.

As educational theory and research uphold that learning is highly impactful when people are doing, rather than learning by listening or observing (Pearce, 2016), this activity allows for the modeling of best practice. Additionally, the "Six Objects Task" can be the basis for a discussion on what elements of a learning experience make it "playful" and what impact playful learning has on student engagement and motivation. Furthermore, the "Six Objects Task" demonstrates that impactful does not always mean elaborate or expensive; sometimes the simplest tasks and the simplest materials can be deeply engaging, playful, and educationally worthwhile. That alone is an excellent lesson for ECE teachers!

Further, because the "Six Objects Task" can be broken down in terms of almost all academic subjects (e.g., emergent literacy, mathematics, science, social studies, art, etc.), it can be used to discuss ways of teaching individual content through play-based methods and as an example of an integrated curriculum approach to ECE. Open-ended, play-based ways to foster learning in individual academic areas can be explored through reflective discussion at the conclusion of the activity (i.e., "What math concepts/skills did we use and practice during the design tasks? What opportunities for science learning happened during the design tasks?"). Another content-specific approach the "Six Objects Task" can introduce is the integrated curriculum approach, applying methodology and language from more than one academic area to examine a central theme, issue, problem, topic, or experience (see review in Michigan Department of Education, 2014).

Fostering Creativity

Today, the field of education, including early childhood, is buzzing with the need for students to not only master foundational academic subjects, but to also gain "twenty-first-century skills," otherwise known as transversal competence. These skills often include learning to learn (including persistence and grit), creativity, critical thinking and problem-solving, interpersonal skills, intrapersonal skills, global citizenship, and media and information literacy (UNESCO Asia-Pacific, 2014; Marsh et al., 2017). Some ways creativity is fostered in teacher preparation include instruction about the connection between play and creativity; creativity as an important "twenty-first-century skill"; creative design and arts-based activities (CDAA) in fostering cross-curricular learning; and CDAA in whole child development, socio-emotional teaching and learning, and transversal competence in young children.

In the context of ECE, transversal competence skills are vital components of social/emotional identity development and a critical factor in educating the "whole child." However, transversal competence is not reserved for children alone; it encompasses many skill sets that are needed when teaching. Therefore, the experiences of ECE teachers need to help teachers both learn about and practice transversal skills themselves, as much as gaining particular ECE content knowledge. In this way, the "Six Objects Task" can serve as both a lived experience and as the center of discussion about the role of, and need for, creative endeavors, along with other transversal skill development opportunities, in early childhood curriculum.

ECE STEM/STEAM Education

Despite the emphasis in many early childhood education traditions on creativity and making things, this has not always been connected explicitly to early STEM education or utilized to form a theoretical grounding for ECE STEM education. Some frames of understanding STEM/STEAM in ECE are instruction on the importance of creativity and art in early STEM/STEAM learning; teaching engineering and design-based thinking to young children; and constructivist theory and makerspace pedagogy applied to ECE settings.

Additionally, the value and use of "A" (Art) in early STEM education remains under debate (Jolly, 2014) and further, the "E" in STEM, as an explicit focus of early childhood teaching, has often been missing in practice. The "Six Objects Task" can be used to jump-start a discussion on each of the aspects and connections between disciplines in STEAM, as well as provide a concrete example of emphasizing the "A" and the "E" in STEAM for student learning. Moreover, a strong focus on design thinking and complex problem-solving during teachers' professional development can improve their capabilities to manage students during designing and making projects, and to help support needed foundational STEM concept and skill development in young children (Early Childhood STEM Working Group, 2017; Marsh et al., 2017).

Furthermore, the "Six Objects Task" can be used to introduce and discuss Piaget's constructivist and Seymour Papert's constructionism ideologies in relation to early STEM/STEAM education; both of these share the connotation of learning as building knowledge structures, with constructionism emphasizing the critical skill of actually physically building (external) as the means of constructing knowledge (internal) (Papert & Harel, 1991).

The "Six Objects Task" can also be used to highlight makerspace pedagogy, which is currently underused as a guide in ECE STEM/STEAM education. This pedagogical approach focuses on the complex set of socially and materially mediated practices that encompass processes of creating artifacts supported by a wide range of STEM-related knowledge and skills, as well as the emotional, relational, and cultural processes surrounding their use and construction (Marsh et al., 2017). During a reflective discussion, participants can examine how the types and amount of materials available during the "Six Objects Task" impacted what they did and created, how different groupings affected their work during the activity, and how this all relates to STEM/STEAM knowledge and skill development.

Example of the "Six Objects Task" in Action

During a discussion in a fall semester undergraduate course on play and learning, a professor suggested that all those October and Halloween art activities (e.g., teacher-cut pumpkins that children glue pre-cut face pieces or glitter onto) were not art, and did not foster creativity or even much thinking. The preservice teachers challenged back, "Yeah, so, what can we *do* besides the cut-out pumpkins if we have a fall theme?" The next class, the professor engaged the students in the "Six Objects Task" using orange play dough and black yarn for a connector.

Unsurprisingly, just the color choice of connectors alone produced various Halloween- and fall-inspired designs from the preservice teachers without any explicit instructor direction or prompting. Using the "Six Objects Task" in the context of Halloween may lead to a serious discussion about the nature of art in relation to thematic teaching in ECE and of how much an impact early childhood teacher's choice of materials and activity influences the opportunities young children have for playful engagement and creative thinking.

CONCLUSION

ECE courses, particularly those focused on curriculum development and play-based pedagogical approaches, often speak to the idea that impactful practice is teaching and learning through *active engagement* of students. The "Six Objects Task," because it allows preservice teachers to be both physically and mentally engaged at an adult level, offers teachers an opportunity for real engagement that many hands-on yet "pretend to be a child" scenarios do not. This, along with both the general reliability of student responses during the activity and the wide range of reflective discussions that can be based on the "Six Objects Task," makes it a particularly impactful practice to use for various ECE teacher preparation concepts.

RECOMMENDED RESOURCES

Lively Minds—Distinctions between Academic vs. Intellectual Goals for Young Children: https://deyproject.files.wordpress.com/2015/04/dey-lively-minds-4-8-15.pdf
Helping Others Understand Academic Rigor in Teachers' Developmentally Appropriate Practice: https://deyproject.files.wordpress.com/2015/04/dey-lively-minds-4-8-15.pdf
The Premature Death of the Whole-Child Approach in Preschool: https://www.brookings.edu/blog/education-plus-development/2017/06/08/the-premature-death-of-the-whole-child-approach-in-preschool/
Educare and Educere: Is a Balance Possible in the Educational System?: https://files.eric.ed.gov/fulltext/EJ724880.pdf
Design Thinking Model: https://www.interaction-design.org/literature/article/5-stages-in-the-design-thinking-process
STEM Smart Brief: http://successfulstemeducation.org/resources/teaching-and-learning-under-next-generation-science-standards
Early STEM Matters: http://d3lwefg3pyezlb.cloudfront.net/docs/Early_STEM_Matters_FINAL.pdf
STEM Starts Early: https://joanganzcooneycenter.org/wp-content/uploads/2017/01/jgcc_stemstartsearly_final.pdf
What is STEAM?: https://educationcloset.com/steam/what-is-steam/

BIBLIOGRAPHY

Blikstein, Paulo. (2013). Digital fabrication and "making" in education: The democratization of invention. *FabLabs: Of machines, makers and inventors*, 4, 1–21.
Early Childhood STEM Working Group. (2017). Early STEM matters: Providing high-quality STEM experiences for all young learners. Chicago: UChicago STEM Education and Erikson Institute.
González, Norma, Moll, Luis C., & Amanti, Cathy (eds.). (2005). *Funds of knowledge: Theorizing practices in households, communities, and classrooms*. New York: Routledge.
Jolly, Anne. (2014). STEM vs. STEAM: Do the arts belong. *Education Week*, 18, 16.
Marsh, Jackie, Kumpulainen, Kristiina, Nisha, Bobby, Velicu, Anca, Blum-Ross, Alicia, Hyatt, David, & Jónsdóttir, Svanborg R. et al. (2017). Makerspaces in the early years: A literature review. Makey Project, University of Sheffield.
Michigan Department of Education. (2014). Curriculum integration research: Re-examining outcomes and possibilities for the 21st century. Lansing: Michigan Department of Education Improvement and Innovation.

Papert, Seymour, & Harel, Idit. (1991). Situating constructionism. *Constructionism, 36*(2), 1–11.
Pearce, Sarah. (2016). Authentic learning: What, why and how. Retrieved from http://www.acel.org.au/acel/ACEL_docs/Publications/e-Teaching/2016/e-Teaching_2016_10.pdf
Roth, Wolff-Michael, & Jornet, Alfredo. (2013). Situated cognition. *Wiley Interdisciplinary Reviews: Cognitive Science, 4*(5), 463–478.
UNESCO Asia-Pacific. (2014). Education policy brief #2: Skills for holistic human development. Retrieved from http://www.unescobkk.org/fileadmin/user_upload/epr/PDF/Policy_Brief_Vol2-28_Nov.pdf
Vygotsky, Lev S. (1978). *Mind in society: The development of higher psychological processes.* Cambridge, MA: Harvard University Press.

Chapter Eleven

Seeking to Create Tech-Savvy Teachers

Lisa L. Minicozzi

Beth and Lori share reflections about recent lessons in their field experiences. Beth explains that she's been placed in an integrated kindergarten classroom with a lead teacher, teaching assistant, and 16 students. Lori works alongside a special education teacher in a self-contained second-grade classroom with nine students. Both teachers work in schools that have one-to-one initiatives, whereby iPads are given to students for classroom learning.

The professor greets the class and asks the group to take out their iPads. Beth shakes her head and says, "I just do not get it . . . every time I'm in the kids want to play on the iPad, but to me, it seems like a glorified worksheet." As Lori is about to respond, the other preservice students in the class adjust their chairs and show interest in the comment. One after another, classmates jump into the conversation, "The school I'm in has a stack of iPads on a table, but the teacher isn't sure how to use them effectively." Another said, "I keep hearing about these one-to-one initiatives around this area, but I worry about how much they expect new teachers to know."

Finally, Lori asks a question, "Professor, why aren't we practicing more with this technology before we get into our own classrooms? What if we get hired by a school that uses them?"

The problems identified by current teacher candidates enrolled in early childhood preservice programs demonstrate the many questions novice teachers have regarding technology use in early learning, P–2 classrooms. It is incumbent upon today's teacher education programs to prepare candidates to integrate technology into classroom learning experiences in order to enhance all student learning outcomes. Schools throughout the nation continue to utilize various forms of technology, such as the iPad or tablet, as essential teaching tools—therefore teacher education programs must learn how to use and teach technology integration to their teacher candidates.

This chapter demonstrates how a teacher education program can integrate technology, specifically iPads, into a methods course to create an impactful practice. This practice not only benefits the teacher education program but also allows teacher candidates to develop skills, expertise, and teaching strategies to better facilitate student learning.

As a means to provide an understanding of this impactful practice (integrating iPads), the following types of examples are explained: shared lesson-planning ideas, anecdotes from class discussions, and collaborative learning practices. Voices from the field are highlighted throughout the chapter to offer readers contextual understanding. The purpose of this chapter is to share the process and outcomes of integrating technology into a teacher education program.

BUILDING THE TECHNOLOGY INFRASTRUCTURE—STEP 1

Faculty need to have the necessary resources to integrate technology into classroom learning experiences. Faculty should begin by asking, What is the feasibility of including innovative technologies into current coursework? For instance, Are there enough iPads for all students? Most faculty have resources (grants) and access to iPads or tablet technology. When considering how to make use of this technology, it is essential to review the logistics of procuring the iPads, managing their use, and understanding any policies or procedures related to these devices.

The widespread adoption and use of iPads as learning tools has brought some technological and pedagogical challenges to the forefront. One pressing challenge continues to be the learning gap between faculty and students. Three areas that need to be addressed in training include 1) learning about a new operating system, 2) device utility, and 3) software applications. Having the necessary supports in place allows faculty as well as teacher candidates to gain confidence in their ability to teach. Providing faculty with experiences to build technological competencies early leads to better modeling and application of the technology.

A first step is collaborating with the information technology department at the university to help guide decision-making throughout the process. Second, faculty need time to practice and develop proficiency with iPads or tablets in order to be able to use these devices with ease. Having faculty learn together with a working group expert, along with a technology expert, helps take away insecurities about effectively using the technology and promotes confidence for individuals to integrate the technology into coursework.

ALIGNING STANDARDS AND PRACTICES—STEP 2

Teacher education programs are forever in the process of making sure coursework aligns with standards. This tends to be a little more of a challenge with regard to technology because of the constant evolution of software and hardware as well as pedagogy within the pre-K–12 field. Considering that challenge, the faculty worked to revise course objectives to meet twenty-first-century learning goals. By aligning the International Society for Technology in Education (ISTE) standards with individual course learning objectives, faculty can begin to look critically at the knowledge and skills needed to best prepare candidates to successfully integrate technology into classroom practice. As the early childhood faculty at our university began to unpack their syllabi, a central question emerged: Do the teacher candidates know how to incorporate iPad technologies in rich and meaningful ways?

Innovative devices can be highly engaging learning tools, but only if educators know how to use them purposefully, which means committing classroom learning toward that goal. After initial discussions with our preservice teachers, it was decided to offer them at least 30 minutes per class, to have hands-on opportunities to explore, create, and problem-solve together. Time to explore technology was paired with the use of critical reflection as part of the experiential learning. Candidates begin to make autonomous classroom decisions, leading to their ability to challenge traditional pedagogical methods, which is a major emphasis is the development of educational technology. Fostering critical reflection within the context of the digital era is an essential aspect of bridging the divide between theoretical understanding and contemporary classroom practices.

EMBEDDING IPADS IN THE COURSE

Through coursework experiences, teacher educators can regularly model how to integrate iPads or other technology into lessons effectively. Modeling initial demonstrations of its use in class is a good starting place. Show candidates the communication capabilities of the technology; in the case of iPads, there is the camera feature, voice-to-text software applications, and Google Classroom (global) connections. It is critical that both educators and candidates explore how a particular technology could enhance learning for all students.

With iPads as the technology, candidates typically spend the first weeks of the semester experimenting with the camera and video features to generate digital stories of their learning journey. In doing so, the multimedia application for sharing thoughts and ideas is seen as a part of collaborative classroom practice. Digital storytelling is one example of an activity in which this can occur. Candidates can download a storytelling app (Book Creator) to use either individually or in a small group to demonstrate understanding. Using the Book Creator app allows students to add text, record voices, and import images and pictures. This activity is great for building basic technology competencies through a shared learning activity.

Discussions focusing on improving teacher preparation should underscore the relevance of using content, pedagogy, and technology to meet the needs of students. Sometimes, in-class discussions between teacher candidates and faculty lead to the recognition of gaps existing between what is happening in partnering school districts and what candidates need to know to be successful in these field-site experiences. Faculty find themselves needing to make their pedagogy relevant based on the technological skillset occurring in classrooms where teacher candidates are placed.

One approach to technology integration by faculty might be a coordinated approach with the local school and community partners. Collaboration among professionals in the field and the university ensures greater synchronization effectiveness in various contexts. This strategy moves learning from being surface level to in-depth and critical. Scheduling regular or bimonthly partnership meetings and field-site observations creates opportunities for planning and executing more effective lessons, as well as keeps the most current technology in view. Preservice teachers continuously work with faculty and mentors to modify coursework to include relevant technology practices, such as aligning local content standards with ISTE standards.

When considering redesigning technology in coursework, effective technology integration must be emphasized. *Effective* technology integration situates technology as supporting curricular goals. Learning and pedagogy are at the center of the design, not the technology. Providing students with opportunities to design lessons while embedding the use of technology (e.g., iPads) will help candidates develop technological pedagogical content knowledge (TPACK) (Koehler & Mishra, 2009; Mishra & Koehler, 2006). The key here is to ask the candidates to think deeply about the role of technology in lesson planning and then support their efforts with in-class discussions and activities. Preservice teachers need to consider how innovative technologies can be used to best accomplish and support instructional goals.

Technology sometimes becomes relevant when teacher candidates work with students with disabilities. One example of this occurred when a teacher candidate who was working with a student with a learning disability designed a persuasive writing lesson for students in a second-grade inclusion classroom. Students first recorded themselves delivering an argument and were then asked to share their recordings with a partner. As reported by the candidate, "Having the ability to see yourself on tape really got these kids engaged in the process of writing a persuasive essay. . . . They talked about their body language, voice, and delivery." Technology used for a lesson in context provided students with an opportunity to work collaboratively, practice verbal communication, and develop social skills.

Integrating the iPad into this lesson allowed for greater student involvement and a positive classroom dynamic. The teacher candidate expressly stated, "I was shocked at how easy it was for the kids to use. . . . They were so happy every day to grab it and begin their writing. . . . My kids are hard to keep on track . . . having the iPad facilitated the lesson and made it fun for the kids to learn . . . and I had fewer meltdowns than usual." Having the opportunity to practice integrating technology while participating in a methodology course fosters understanding and readiness to integrate that technology into one's daily teaching (Minicozzi, 2018).

METHODS 2.0 — STEP 3

Integrating technology into a methods course leads to the following question: What does the course redesign look like? The methods course now embraces a collaborative workshop model. Each week, candidates work together in small groups or pairings to build knowledge through shared learning experiences. Methods course experiences feature the following: exploration of iPad functionality (hardware capabilities, camera/video features), exploration of software applications (finding and evaluating student learning apps based on learning domains and content), designing P–2 lesson plans, working on collaborative lesson plans, revisions with mentor teachers at field sites, alignment activities (student learning outcomes with technology integration linked to content-related standards), and reflections. Preservice teachers are asked to develop an individual, differentiated lesson plan including iPad integration as a learning tool. Throughout the lesson planning process, candidates are asked to consider if they can use the iPad instruction in a way that meaningfully contributes to the learning objectives.

One of the learning objectives for technology is to get educators to continually explore the value and purpose of educational apps for pre-K–12 learners. In methods courses, candidates can explore specific apps and the meaning each brings to the learning experience. For example, teacher candidates create a working list of iPad applications they find to be most useful for students, and then categorize the apps into the following groupings: literacy, math, writing, and creation.

Throughout the semester, candidates add to the list and discuss how to utilize the apps for meeting individual student learning goals. Some of the teacher candidates have described positive student learning outcomes after integrating the One Minute Read app into K–1 literacy lessons, specifically during independent reading time. According to the candidates, students like the ease and intuitive nature of the app's three-stage process. The app itself provides immediate feedback for learners, which fosters engagement and willingness to continue working on the assigned activity.

Preservice teachers spend time each week during the course reviewing the developmental appropriateness of literacy as well as other content-based learning apps. They often pair up and explore how an app might support a combination of literacy skills such as reading, writing, speaking, and listening. By incorporating technology (i.e., iPads, tablets) into a methods course as an impactful practice, candidates have an opportunity to explore the range of pedagogical strategies the technology offers diverse learners. Candidates have in-class and field-site opportunities to create and enact lesson plans, which showcase their content knowledge, instructional strategies, and ability to teach with technology.

EMBRACE CHALLENGES—STEP 4

Identifying challenges early on has value in creating opportunities for improvement in the design of teacher education programming. In this case, it was the early childhood program, and the following questions needed to be considered when thinking about technology integration: What are the program's overall goals and objectives? Does the program have a capacity for change? Can innovative technologies be used as a learning tool? If so, how? Engaging in reflective dialogue helps frame how the methods course could be redesigned.

Although the national trend has been to increase technology use across P–12 educational settings, there are specific obstacles to achieving this goal in early childhood classrooms. Teachers of young children are concerned with the appropriateness of technology integration in early learning settings (Blackwell et al., 2014; NAEYC, 1996). Since the Academy of Pediatrics (Council on Communications, 2013) recommends limited screen time for children ages three to eight and no screen time for children under two, some educators question the place and value of technology (iPads) in early childhood settings. Many teachers and parents speculate about the developmental and socioemotional drawbacks of technology on children's learning.

Accepted early childhood pedagogical practices have always included an emphasis on the development of the whole child (socially/emotionally, physically, cognitively), through play-based learning experiences. Traditionally early childhood teachers have placed little emphasis on technology-based skills. Having conversations about how to navigate technology is important; for our program, this occurred through joint discussions with our field-site mentor teachers. Potential issues related to developmentally appropriate practices and technology in early childhood have been addressed as a collaborative process.

Research indicates that when early childhood teachers are actively involved (asking questions, prompting responses, fostering collaboration) when using classroom technology, students make gains in cognitive, literacy, math, and language domains (McMannis & Gunnewig, 2012; Penuel et al., 2009). The National Association for the Education of Young Children (NAEYC) and the Fred Rogers Center for Early Learning and Children's Media at Saint Vincent College, in a joint position statement, explain that technology integration can contribute to an improved support of individual learning goals (2012). The position statement emphasizes that integrating technology into any P–2 learning experience should be done with care and concern, allowing children to explore, create, and problem-solve. While professional organizations provide guidance for learning, it is also important for teacher candidates to not feel overly prescribed to when they are attempting to create authentic learning experiences.

As teacher preparation programs in early childhood begin to make shifts to include more technology-rich experiences for candidates, it is suggested to have preservice teachers think through developmentally appropriate practices with technology integration. Working in small groups and focusing on one content area for an extended period of time (in this case, literacy) has helped candidates get a sense of how the iPad can work to support skill development while embracing the whole child. The same developmentally appropriate practices that have always guided teachers in making choices for materials and instructional strategies apply to the integration of technology. Faculty at our university attempt to support candidates at all stages of teacher development as they develop knowledge embrace critical reflection, and infuse practice with emerging understandings of digital learning.

FINDING A HIGH-QUALITY PARTNER—STEP 5

While redesign influences internal programmatic change, full utility of technology integration occurs when colleges and universities redefine how their partnerships function with local stakeholders (i.e., school districts, childcare centers, and after school programs). In order for practical experiences to positively impact student learning, the role of the cooperating mentor teachers is crucial. Having a solid understanding of the expectations candidates face in their field-site settings allows the transition from theory to practice.

Sometimes, faculty work to provide their partner district with needed professional development opportunities (i.e., in the area of emergent literacy practices). Workshops and professional learning opportunities for community partners strengthen the relationship between mentor teachers and university faculty. As well, there is an increased perception of investment in the partnership.

In addition, university partners offer collaborative research opportunities in a *joint* effort to improve student learning. Currently, faculty members co-teach with affiliate school mentor teachers. Having the opportunity to collaborate with partners opens the door for improved communication, which creates a shared responsibility for teacher preparation. As partners work together, they gain clarity on clinical expectations for teacher candidates. In doing so, university faculty are able to make course revisions that better reflect the demands of the fieldwork contexts in which our preservice teachers will practice. Building more authentic and field-based learning experiences for teacher candidates can ultimately improve their willingness to take risks and pioneer new teaching tools, such as digital (iPad) technologies.

Research has indicated a strong link between a teacher's decision to use technology in the classroom and the barriers they may face in doing so. Teachers' attitudes and beliefs often play a critical role in whether candidates can integrate new technologies into daily practice (Burden & Hopkins, 2016; Ertmer, 1999; 2005). Therefore, providing candidates with varied and practical field-based opportunities might influence their fundamental beliefs and attitudes about the value of technology and learning.

Having teacher candidates draft and enact technology as part of a holistic process ending with the implementation of lesson plans within the context of the learning (coursework) environment deepens pedagogical knowledge and skills. While the basic fear of technology is no longer a barrier, internal insecurities may still "impede meaningful use" of technology for classroom learning (Burden & Hopkins, 2016; Ertmer, 1999; Park & Ertmer, 2007). Today's teacher candidates need direct classroom experiences, working alongside mentor teachers to develop skills and knowledge in order to understand what meaningful technology integration looks like in a P–2 setting.

LESSONS LEARNED

Relevant recommendations certainly include the need for technology integration throughout current pedagogical coursework to better prepare P–2 teachers. Underscoring the importance of collaboration as an impactful practice can lead to continuous improvement for teacher education and our collective responsibility to prepare skilled educators. The iPad is but one evolving piece of technology and should be considered within the broader context of constructivist practices. The intention of our early childhood program is to develop candidates' knowledge and be able to use a comprehensive approach (including technology) to develop high-quality student learning embedded with creative, innovative, and collaborative experiences.

Teacher education programs must ensure clear alignment of goals and objectives with the technology-driven curricular shifts adopted by affiliate school districts. Based on our initial efforts, it is suggested that teacher preparation programs regularly review course offerings with local partnership school professionals and mentors to ensure alignment as a means to further develop candidates' knowledge, confidence, and pedagogical skill.

The context of integrating technology as a way to make university coursework and field experiences relevant is obvious when it happens. One teacher candidate responded, "Wow, I never knew the iPad could be used this way." She further commented, "I see the strength of the app is in its simplicity." The value of this snippet reminds teacher educators of the importance of staying relevant. By providing teacher candidates with course-related opportunities to practice and hone TPACK skills, greater understanding and readiness to integrate technology will be fostered. Teacher candidates require time and technology-rich learning experiences in order to develop skills and expertise for developmentally appropriate technology integration.

FINAL THOUGHTS

After the completion of their student teaching experiences, candidates returned to the campus to offer insights into finding full-time teaching positions. Cate announced, "I can't believe I'm already working . . . it's all because of the connection to Franklin Gardens [an affiliate school district]." She further commented, "Having the close relationship our supervisor has with the principal and teachers really helped shape my experiences and prepare me to successfully teach in their first-grade classrooms. I knew what programs they used and felt comfortable teaching in a 1:1 school [with iPads]."

The faculty continually use student feedback to inform how they teach and design effective preparation experiences to benefit the teacher candidates. It remains vital that the faculty embrace the fieldwork partners and stay up-to-date on classroom learning endeavors. Engaging today's learners requires ongoing modifications to match the needs of all students. Integrating innovative tablet technology is just another tool for differentiating instruction. Welcome the chance to explore, innovate, and create—beyond the campus borders—so that the next generation of teachers will do the same.

Collaboration among educators is a vital component for improved candidate learning outcomes. Being more intentional about the quality of experiences candidates have during their preservice training can support innovations in the field of teaching. By working together with field-site partners, efforts are focused on practical teaching experiences grounded in research and supported by university faculty, and mentor teachers. Schools of education benefit when P–2 education systems challenge them to change. As faculty members consider integrating innovative technologies into coursework, they can also be inspired by new dialogue that embraces teaching in the twenty-first century.

Teaming with partner schools offers innovative professional opportunities for both novice and veteran teachers. Having university educators working directly with mentor teachers and teacher candidates can ensure more consistent expectations for their development. Although the core of what faculty teach has not significantly changed, how the faculty teach certainly has—teacher preparation programs should continually reflect the complexities of contemporary education.

BIBLIOGRAPHY

Battaglia, Dana, Curringa, Mathew, Minicozzi, Lisa, Vaughn-Shavo, Faith, McCarthy, Mary Jean, & Zarco, Emilia Patricia. (2015). From laptop to tablet: Faculty use of iPads for instruction to prepare education professionals. *Excelsior: Leadership in Teaching and Learning*, 17.

Blackwell, Courtney. (2013). Teacher practices with mobile technology integrating tablet computers into the early childhood classroom. *Journal of Education Research*, 7(4), 231–255.

Blackwell, Courtney K., Lauricella, Alexis R., & Wartella, Ellen. (2014). Factors influencing digital technology use in early childhood education. *Computers & Education*, 77, 82–90.

Burden, Kevin, & Hopkins, Paul. (2016). Barriers and challenges facing pre-service teachers use of mobile technologies for teaching and learning. In Information Resources Management Association, *Blended learning: Concepts, methodologies, tools, and applications*. Hershey, PA: IGI Global, 1665–1686.

Council on Communications. (2013). Children, adolescents, and the media. *Pediatrics*, 132(5), 958.

Dias, Lina, & Victor, Angelin. (2017). Teaching and learning with mobile devices in the 21st century digital world: Benefits and challenges. *European Journal of Multidisciplinary Studies*, 2(5), 339–344.

Ertmer, Peggy A. (1999). Addressing first-and second-order barriers to change: Strategies for technology integration. *Educational Technology Research and Development*, 47(4), 47–61.

Ertmer, Peggy A. (2005). Teacher pedagogical beliefs: The final frontier in our quest for technology integration? *Educational Technology Research and Development*, 53(4), 25–39.

Koehler, Matthew J., Zellner, Andrea L., Roseth, Cary J., Dickson, Robin K., Dickson, W. Patrick, & Bell, John. (2013). Introducing the first hybrid doctoral program in educational technology. *TechTrends*, 57(3), 47–53.

Koehler, Matthew, & Mishra, Punya. (2009). What is technological pedagogical content knowledge (TPACK)? *Contemporary Issues in Technology and Teacher Education*, 9(1), 60–70.

McManis, Lilla Dale, & Gunnewig, Susan B. (2012). "=Finding the education in educational technology with early learners. *Young Children*, 67(3), 14–24.

Minicozzi, Lisa L. (2018). iPads and pre-service teaching: Exploring the use of iPads in k–2 classrooms. *International Journal of Information and Learning Technology*, 35(3), 160–180.

Mishra, Punya, & Koehler, Matthew J. (2006). Technological pedagogical content knowledge: A framework for teacher knowledge. *Teachers College Record*, 108(6), 1017–1054.

National Association for the Education of Young Children. (1996). NAEYC position statement: Technology and young children—ages three through eight. *Young Children*, 51(6), 11–16.

National Association for the Education of Young Children and the Fred Rogers Center for Early Learning and Children's Media. (2012). Technology and interactive media as tools in early childhood programs serving children from birth through age 8.

Park, Sung Hee, & Ertmer, Peggy A. (2007). Impact of problem-based learning (PBL) on teachers' beliefs regarding technology use. *Journal of Research on Technology in Education, 40*(2), 247–267.

Penuel, William R., Pasnik, Shelley, Bates, Lauren, Townsend, Eve, Gallagher, Lawrence P., Llorente, Carlin, & Hupert, Naomi. (2009). *Preschool teachers can use a media-rich curriculum to prepare low-income children for school success: Results of a randomized controlled trial*. Newton, MA: Education Development Center and SRI.

Shulman, Lee S. (1987). Knowledge and teaching: Foundations of the new reform. *Harvard Educational Review, 57*, 1–22.

Chapter Twelve

Using Online Teacher Education Preparation as a Way to Diversify the Early Childhood Teaching Force

Billi L. Bromer

The diverse student body that populates twenty-first-century classrooms requires teachers who emerge from a variety of backgrounds, cultures, and experiences. Sources of diversity in the early childhood teaching force include skilled adults already working with young children, such as paraprofessionals, teacher assistants, or uncertified yet experienced pre-K teachers. This pool of prospective teacher candidates is often unable to enroll in traditional face-to-face college degree and teacher licensure programs because of income, employment, home location, family responsibilities, or other individual needs (Lutton, 2011; Renes & Strange, 2011).

One alternative option being implemented to meet the life needs of these prospective teacher candidates is an online undergraduate educator preparation program. This program has been specifically designed to accommodate nontraditional learners with a process equivalent to the content and comparable learning outcomes found in face-to-face programs.

The online courses described in this chapter utilize the Canvas Learning Management System (Canvas Learning Management System, n.d.) and depend on technology. Also vital to the success of the online format is the expertise of the instructors, especially their ability to transfer the dispositional attributes of engagement and enthusiasm to virtual interactions. Essential to this design is a commitment to believing that when online pedagogy is approached in a critical manner it can be equally as effective as more traditional forms of teacher preparation.

To assure that quality is met, approaches should be consistent with evidence-based and professionally agreed upon practices. This chapter describes examples of online courses and strategies that are used to prepare teachers who are culturally responsive, technology skilled, and possess the collaborative skills needed for twenty-first-century teaching. Online coursework, as an impactful practice, has the potential to help individuals already part of pre-K–5 schooling move into a more empowered position as a licensed teacher while respecting their challenges and obstacles that prevent them from participating in a more traditional program.

PREPARING CULTURALLY RESPONSIVE TEACHERS

Preparing future teachers who recognize and appreciate the diversity of their students across races, cultures, classes, genders, and other parameters can emerge from a range of teacher preparation experiences. The very fact that online students may come from regionally diverse areas of the state in itself makes every conversation among online students in all courses rich and varied. As students share their own unique experiences and backgrounds, a meaningful exploration of regional differences emerges. Culturally responsive teaching occurs through a multicultural education course, which highlights an attitude inventory assignment.

Multicultural Education Course

An online course in multicultural education provides students with a broad perspective on the racial, cultural, and ethnic diversity of the children they will teach. The course "Introduction to Multicultural Education" is an opportunity for students to examine issues of race, ethnicity, gender, and culture as they occur in today's classrooms. Within an online format, all students must engage in conversations around unconscious beliefs about privilege, values, and social justice; student bias, as well as their sense of advocacy, emerge authentically in a space where no one can hide their thoughts.

Students are encouraged to examine the beliefs and behaviors that may relate to prejudice, racism, gender bias, and cultural insensitivity. Several assignments in the course are transformational as students become aware of their own attitudes and reflect on how innate ideas may affect their teaching. A particularly impactful assignment is an attitude inventory that students access online both at the beginning and the end of the course.

Students are required to complete a questionnaire found on the Canvas Learning Management System. In the attitude inventory assignment, students assess their thinking about race, class, and gender by indicating "Strongly Agree," "Agree," "Undecided," "Disagree," or "Strongly Disagree" for 75 statements. The following are examples of those statements:

- *Racial segregation in schools and neighborhoods remains a problem.*

- *Poverty today is a problem primarily affecting children.*
- *All occupations should be open to both men and women.*

The instructor shares collective results as a means to stimulate and challenge student beliefs. As students gain insight into their beliefs on race, class, and gender, learning starts to delve deeper into discussions on specific topics, such as racism and a legacy of white domination, sexism as personal and political, gender identity in today's society, different ability rather than disability, pluralism in a changing society, and multiculturalism in twenty-first-century classrooms.

Students exchange thoughts on a wide range of topics that may challenge their personal opinions but that are also vital to understanding their own potential biases. After again completing the inventory at the end of the course, students must reflect on what they have learned about themselves and others as it pertains to race, class, and gender. Outcomes of the post-test inventory and essay reflection show that students attain the critical objective of developing an awareness of how their attitudes toward other cultures can influence behavior in and out of the classroom.

PREPARING TECHNOLOGY SKILLED TEACHERS

Twenty-first-century teaching embraces technology and requires teachers to instruct and assess students using digital resources (Caywood & Duckett, 2003). The infusion of technology in early childhood education has created a growing need for educator preparation programs to develop teacher competencies in technology that are linked to instruction. Online coursework functions both as an instructional tool for learning in the teacher preparation course and also as a model for future educators to experience as a tool for learning technology pedagogy.

A dedicated course in instructional technology, in which two challenging assignments teach skills that can be used directly in teaching, is easily—if not better—attained online. The two key assignments are especially impactful not only because they challenge students but also because they build student confidence and reduce technology apprehension. The podcast assignment and the web page assignment are explained next.

Podcast Assignment

In the podcast assignment, students must prepare a well-organized script that is about five minutes long. It could be a story that can be played by a young child's family at home or a mini-lesson on a topic such as the life cycle of a butterfly. Podcast creation software is suggested, but students may use any other software they prefer. Through the assignment, candidates are encouraged to use technology to develop content, but it also engages them in applying it directly to instruction.

Requiring students to develop a voice podcast on any topic for a grade level they prefer is an assignment that excites and motivates them to apply technology in their own teaching. With the influx of iPads or tablets in classrooms or a "bring your own device" approach in some schools, knowing how to create online content and use it in instruction is a highly useful skill for candidates to acquire. In fact, the idea of using technology to design learning to meet the needs of students while preparing them for twenty-first-century learning is the definition of innovation.

Web Page Assignment

In the web page assignment, students are required to develop their own web site using Google Sites web-hosting service. Students then add their podcast to the web page they have prepared. Uploads up to 10 MB are permitted, so students must be sure that their podcast—with any other files, photos, documents, and so forth, that they choose to add to the web page—does not exceed the limit.

Social media has become a common tool for communication among teachers, students, and parents in early childhood classrooms. Although teachers may choose not to communicate with students on popular social media sites, schools use web sites to link the school community to parents. Having already created their own web sites, candidates come to their professional roles ready to do so in whatever school they may join.

PREPARING TEACHERS WHO CAN COLLABORATE

The ability to collaborate effectively with others is a vital teacher skill that occurs naturally in a face-to-face course. Whether students prefer group assignments or not, instructors often use them to encourage the development of the skills needed to work and plan together as a part of preparing them for the teaching profession. It's possible to move desks or tables to create small groups for discussions or work on assignments together in a face-to-face course. This is a more significant challenge in an online course. One successful way group work occurs online is through a small group presentation assignment utilizing Canvas.

Online Class Presentation Assignment

In a developmental psychology course, where educational theories are studied, students are randomly placed in small groups of four or five to research a specific learning theory. They must work as a group to produce a 20-minute

PowerPoint (PPT) presentation on the particular theory the group has been assigned. Collaboration occurs through students utilizing technology to communicate with each other in various forms as well as using the technology to create the PPT.

Students can easily collaborate online in a web meeting option available in the course and can prepare the presentation using Google Docs as well as their course site. To encourage and also oversee student collaboration, the author has found that providing separate discussion boards for each small group of students is helpful. Students can plan their assignment and discuss each person's role in developing the PPT slides. The instructor is a member of each small group discussion board to be able to answer questions about the assignment and—in some cases when needed—redirect a reluctant group member to engage in the group project.

Toward the end of the course, a synchronous online class session is scheduled using Zoom video conferencing (Zoom, n.d.), available in the Canvas course, and each group must present their PPT to the entire class. Screen sharing directly available in Zoom enables all students to view the PPT while group members take turns providing the information in their slides. Although students may be apprehensive about working with others on one common assignment, the author has found that students exhibit excitement at the opportunity to learn from each other in a synchronous class session.

Online Courses Support Technology Comfortable Candidates

The courses and strategies highlighted in the chapter show that it is possible to prepare students who are culturally responsive and able to collaborate effectively through an online teacher preparation program. Moreover, with preparing students who are technology skilled—the third indicator of an effective program—an online program may actually be more successful at helping candidates attain those learning outcomes.

A course in instructional technology is a good start, but students must use technology throughout their educator preparation program; they need to learn it and become more confident in using it. Students in online courses are active users rather than passive consumers of technology, and the result of ongoing use is significant. In contrast to a traditional face-to-face program, students in an online program have more opportunities to interact, present assignments, and work collaboratively with peers using technology, and they become more adept in using it.

This is an impactful outcome because technology use becomes more naturally connected to learning, teaching, and communicating. When those educator indicators naturally become part of how candidates function, those abilities transfer more quickly to their professional roles as teachers. With each new web tool learned or technology challenge overcome, students indicate more confidence in using technology with their own future students.

LESSONS LEARNED AND CHANGES MADE

Many lessons have been learned in order to make this online program successful. In the following section two crucial lessons are discussed as a means to make online learning personal: 1) seeing and hearing each other online is essential, and 2) being available to students is essential; so two strategies for doing this are provided.

Seeing and Hearing Each Other Online Is Important

Some people believe that individuals who choose online learning are independent learners and prefer to do their assignments alone, but that is often not the case. The author has learned that online students want to engage with others just as they would do in a face-to-face course and they want to establish some connection to the instructor. The challenge has been in how to create personal connections with students using technology, primarily through a computer.

Students need to hear and see their instructor and each other (Donahue, Fox, & Torrance, 2007; Young & Bruce, 2011). The personal engagement of the instructor with his or her students encourages adult learners to get more deeply involved in their learning (Overstreet, 2018). Just like instructors in face-to-face courses start the course with an icebreaker to have students create personal connections and get to know each other, the same needs to occur during an online course. To make sure that online students are seen and heard, the author has added specific strategies to her courses that have been effective.

Use Audio-Video Introductions

Discussion boards are often the major component of online courses and are included as a way to introduce participants to each other in an online course, but this format can get tedious for all participants to read written introduction after introduction. Combining both audio and video together online is a far more exciting way to introduce class members. Voice Thread is an easy to learn and simple to use web-based program that can be included in Canvas as an added option.

At the start of an online course, the instructor created a Voice Thread assignment and posted her own Voice Thread as a model for students. The instructor added a few photos and an audio greeting to share a bit of personal information about herself with her students. Then using Voice Thread themselves, students upload photos, quotes, poems, add their own words in a narrative, and create their personal audio and video introduction. The instructor and students could also greet each other with a written response that appears as a text message on the students' Voice Threads or as recorded messages that students can play.

The outcome of this approach is a more dynamic start to courses. Not only do students get to talk about themselves and their families or hobbies or anything they choose, they also get to show images and photos that individualize and humanize each student. The author has found this to be an extraordinarily effective way for an instructor to view each student individually and personally rather than just as a name on a roster.

Include Audio-Video Mini-Lectures

The audio and video introductions are a great start, but to create a continuing "classroom experience" in a virtual environment, it's vital to keep the personal connections going, especially between the instructor and each student. In a developmental psychology course in which theories and concepts may be new to students and challenging to understand, weekly mini-lectures help support learning.

PPT slides are modified to become "mini-lectures" through audio explaining each slide in context as a means for clarity. Graphics make the slides clearer and more explicit. The instructor then created a short video of the narration using SnagIt (Techsmith, n.d.). A "mini-lecture" takes a face-to-face approach and is used as an online strategy to engage student learners, helping the instructor come alive to students. Students can listen to the mini-lecture right in the Canvas course on a computer or even on a smartphone using the Canvas app as often as they want.

The author has learned that it is important to keep the mini-lectures short and to the point, no more than 10 to 12 minutes long. It's also useful to highlight essential concepts for students from that week's readings and explain them differently than they might be explained in a textbook. Student feedback notes the effectiveness of this addition in creating a classroom experience, as demonstrated in the following comment: "I enjoyed the mini-lectures given each week. Since I am an online student, it gave me that classroom experience that I am unable to receive daily."

Two Strategies for Being Available to Students

A key lesson learned by the author is that the availability of an instructor during times when online students are more likely to be doing assignments makes a difference to students. It makes a strong impact on student engagement in the course. Students in face-to-face courses are provided faculty office hours, but what "office" does an online student visit? When do students speak with an instructor when they may work all day and do assignments at night? Online students need evening or weekend hours to accommodate work or family obligations. Meeting the needs of online students means offering to be present based on their schedules. Two strategies work well: opening evening chat rooms and providing online web meetings.

The author introduced a chat room that is easily set up in Canvas for an hour or so about one evening per week. Students can "drop in" and "chat" with the instructor at a time when their questions are more likely to arise—at night. Any instructor can simply open up a chat room, just like he or she might open up an office door, and wait for students to enter the room with a question or need for clarification on an assignment. Some students enter the chat to see what others are asking and find that helpful. Some students chat more than others. The author found that instructor effort is small in providing a chat room, but the impact is huge. The ability for students to engage in "real-time" discussion with each other and with the instructor is a highly impactful practice in regards to online problem-solving.

Online instruction in an asynchronous format is definitely the most common and also the most convenient format for nontraditional students, and it does provide flexibility for both the instructor and the learners. For some courses, such as one in lesson planning, a chat room was not enough for issues that might require an example or more details. For a course in which a specific skill—such as writing a lesson plan—is a learning objective, the author added a weekly evening web meeting created in Zoom within the Canvas course.

Zoom video conferencing facilitates screen sharing so that the instructor can provide examples on the screen for students and the conversation can move more quickly than in a written chat. The synchronous class sessions enabled students to discuss elements of the lesson plan assignment directly with the instructor at a time when they might be working on it. Student comments indicated that real-time interaction was beneficial:

> *This course was very helpful and effective for education majors . . . giving feedback and helping us walk step by step through lesson planning through Zoom meetings.*
>
> *I appreciated phone and Zoom meetings that fit into my life of 4 kids, school, and work.*
>
> *I like how interactive it was, especially Zoom meetings every week that would allow us to ask questions.*

The instructor could clarify instructions or counter misconceptions or confusion students might have.

GENUINE CONNECTION MAKES AN ONLINE COURSE IMPACTFUL

The author has learned that student and instructor engagement make all the difference in whether or not an online course is effective and what impact it may have on student learning. The need for "genuine connection" in a course is well explained in the following statement:

> *Even though this was an online course and at times it can be difficult to feel that you are communicating efficiently, I felt that there was a sincere connection and the communications we had were always insightful. I was always hesitant about taking an online class. I thought negatively about the communication or bond that could be achieved through merely speaking through a screen. . . . .I felt that we all brought something to the table and made the class fun as well as interesting. The class itself and the content of it really allowed [me] to feel that there was a genuine connection between all.*

Adding any of the strategies described in the chapter to an existing online course can be beneficial or can be a transitional process to moving a face-to-face course to an online format. When multiple courses are added in an online format, a complete educator preparation program can be developed. The program referenced in this chapter has done that and, as an outcome, the pool of teacher candidates has broadened. A wider candidate pool has created the start of a powerful opportunity to add more diversity to the state's early childhood teaching force.

BIBLIOGRAPHY

Canvas Learning Management System. (n.d.). Canvas. Retrieved from https://www.canvaslms.eu/
Caywood, KayDee, & Duckett, Jane. (2003). Online vs. on-campus learning in teacher education. *Teacher Education and Special Education, 26*(2), 98–105.
Donohue, Chip, Fox, Selena, & Torrence Debra. (2007). Early childhood educators as elearners. *Young Children, 1*(6), 34–40.
Lutton, Alison. (2011). Using the new NAEYC® professional preparation standards. *YC Young Children, 66*(2), 78.
Overstreet, Jennifer. (2018). Rethinking the role of teacher; 3 practices to elevate student engagement. Retrieved from https://www.teachingchannel.org/blog/2018/04/16/rethinking-the-role-of-teacher/?utm_source=newsletter20181027
Renes, Susan L., & Strange, Anthony T (2011). Using technology to enhance higher education. *Innovative Higher Education, 36*(3), 203–213.
Techsmith. (n.d.). The new SnagIt has arrived. Retrieved from https://www.techsmith.com/
Voice Thread. (n.d.). Amazing conversations about media. Retrieved from https://voicethread.com/
Young, Suzanne, & Bruce, Mary Alice. (2011). Classroom community and student engagement in online courses. *Journal of Online Learning and Teaching, 7*(2), 219–230.
Zoom. (n.d.). Zoom. Retrieved from https://zoom.us/

Index

Academy of Pediatrics, 130
active engagement, with ECE STEM/STEAM education, 122
active learning strategies, 67
activity plans, 11; culturally based child rearing practices, 11; exceptionalities relating to, 6–7, 10–11; physical disabilities, 11, 12; role-playing, 11–12, 14; variety of, 11–13
Activity Plan Simulations, 3–4, 6; activity plans for, 11–13; course in foundations and pedagogy for exceptional children, 4–6, 11, 14; group project, 6–7; implementation of, 7–11, 13, 14; lessons learned from, 13–14; presentation with, 7, 13–14
Activity Plan Template, 9, 13
Alfandary, Peter, 38
algorithms, 102, 103, 105
American culture, as normal, 47
antibias curriculum, 55–56
appropriateness: cultural, 37; developmentally appropriate practice, 55–56; of technology infrastructure, 130–131
assignments, vii, 42; guidelines for, 68–70; online class presentation assignment, 140–141; with PLCs, 78; podcast, 139–140; web page, 140
Association of Teacher Educators, vii
audio-video introductions, 142–143

audio-video mini-lectures, 143
awareness, ix–x; cultural, 31, 38–39

Beaumont, Karen, 59
beliefs, transforming of, ix–x. *See also* cultural beliefs visibility, in early childhood teacher education
belonging: toward, 41; building up and breaking down, 48–49; with diverse teaching workforce, 48; Family Immigration Story Project, 41–48; resources for, 49
benefits: of hydroponic gardens, as learning tool, 88; of impactful practices, vii; of mathematics assessment, 99; of "Six Object Task" activity, 111; of video-cued discussions, 34–35
best practices, vii, 35–36
biases, 41, 42, 138, 139
bilingual children, 47
bilingual methodology, 10
blind or visually impaired children, 9–10
Book Creator, 128

Canvas Learning Management System, 137, 141, 142
case studies, with video-cued discussions, 34
CDAA. *See* creative design and arts-based activities
chat rooms, 143–144

"Child, Family, Culture and Community", 42, 47
children: blind or visually impaired, 9–10; cultural and linguistic assets of, 41, 42, 47; discrimination impact on, 41, 47; diverse population of, 53; of first-generation immigrants, 43–44; in preschool and kindergarten, 53. *See also* exceptional children
Children & Nature Network, 87
CLASS. *See* Classroom Assessment Scoring System
class historian assignment guidelines, 68–70
Classroom Assessment Scoring System (CLASS), 6, 8, 10, 13
classrooms: demographic changes in, 31; explorations beyond, 67–68; instruction in, 5–6; normative, culture- and value-free practices in, 32; technology infrastructure for, 126
clinical field experience, with PLCs, 79–80
code-switching, 8
coevalness, 52
collaboration, through shared power, 42
collaborative learning teams, 75–76
collaborative open-ended design and redesign, with "Six Object Task" activity, 115–117
collaborative research opportunities, for tech-savvy teachers, 132
collaborative skills, online teacher education for, 137, 140–141
collaborative workshop model, with technology infrastructure, 129
colleague from school counseling help, with pseudo-conferences, 19–20
Common Core Literacy Standards, 91
Common Core State Standards, for mathematics, 98
communication, 38–39, 127
community: development of, ix–x; learning community, extending of, 67–68
community college courses, 4–6
community of learners, 51; coevalness relating to, 52; compassion, nurturance, love relating to, 53; conclusion to, 60–61; for diverse population of students, 51–52, 53, 54; impactful practice of, 52–57; implementation of, 57–59; lessons learned, 59–60; multicultural perspectives with, 53–54, 55; project for, 56, 57; for PSTs, 18, 51–56; teacher educators relating to, 52–54, 56, 57–59
compassion, 53
competence skills, transversal, 120
competencies, for PSTs, 3, 6, 13
complex open-ended design and redesign, with "Six Object Task" activity, 115–117
composition, of "Six Object Task" activity, 117
Concept Development and Language Modeling, 6
conduction, of "Six Object Task" activity, 113–117
connectedness, 51
course material, engaging with, 67
creating voice, 17; interactions with, 17–18; lessons learned, 26–29; outcomes of, 25–26
creating voice, implementation of, 18; interaction with, 18–19; parent panels, 18, 19, 22–23; preparation for, 19–22; pseudo-conferences, 18, 19, 23–24
creating voice, with student and parent relationship, 17; challenges of, 18; learning experience with, 18; parent panel for, 18; pseudo-conference for, 18
creative design and arts-based activities (CDAA), 120
creativity fostered, with "Six Object Task" activity, 120
cultural and linguistic assets, of children, 41, 42, 47
cultural appropriateness, 37
cultural awareness, 31, 38–39
cultural beliefs visibility, in early childhood teacher education, 31–32; communication relating to, 38–39; impactful practice of, 32–33; lessons learned, 38–39; teacher candidates engaged in culture conversations, 36–37; video-cued discussions for, 32, 33–36
cultural experiences, of teachers, 31–32

culturally based child rearing practices, 11
culturally responsive pedagogy, 14
culturally responsive teachers, 137–139
cultural values, 10–11, 14
culture, 32, 47, 138
culture positioning, 31–32
curriculum: antibias, 55–56; innovation in instruction and, x–xi; Integrated Curriculum, 55–56

DAP. *See* developmentally appropriate practice
data source, vii
"The Day the Crayons Quit", 59
decision-making: processes of, viii; with technology infrastructure, 126
degree program, for early childhood education, vii
democratizing engagement, 52
demographic changes, within classrooms, 31
Design Thinking Model, 118
development: of community, ix–x; of exceptional children, 3; of PSTs, 13–14
developmentally appropriate practice (DAP), 55–56
digital storytelling, with iPads, 127–128
discovery, with hydroponic gardens, 92
discrimination, 41, 47
discussions, 10, 93; in-class, 58–59; for parent panels, 22–23; with PLCs, 80–81; preservice teachers and, 5, 53–54. *See also* video-cued discussions
diverse population: of students, 51–52, 53, 54; of teachers, 48
diversity, 137, 138
dysrhythmic conditions, 52–53

early childhood education (ECE), 88; degree programs for, vii; with Family Immigration Story Project, 41–48; personal biases of, 41, 42; teachers roles in, 41; transformative experiences of, 51, 53. *See also* cultural beliefs visibility, in early childhood teacher education; "Six Object Task" activity
Early Childhood Special Interest Group, vii
ECE. *See* early childhood education

ECE STEM/STEAM education, 117, 120; active engagement with, 122; constructivist ideologies with, 121; pedagogy associated with, 121; understanding of, 120; value and use of, 120
EdTPA, 9
education. *See specific topics*
edutopia.org/blog/rethinking-difficult-parents-allen-mendler, 21
effective practices, vii, 75–76
Ehlert, Lois, 78
emotional responses, 36, 47
empathy, 31–32, 55
empowerment, ix, 18, 26, 27
engagement, 42–43; active, with ECE STEM/STEAM education, 122; democratizing, 52; reflective practice, 71, 72–73; relational, 51; of teacher candidates, in culture conversations, 36–37, 47
environmental education, 87–88
ethnic diversity, 138
evaluations, 78, 81–82
exceptional children, 3, 4–6, 11, 14
exceptionalities, with Activity Plan Simulations, 6–7, 10–11
experiences. *See specific experiences*
experiential learning, with hydroponic gardens, 92
Exploring Sounds and Rhythms of Musical Instruments activity, for blind or visually impaired children, 9–11

facilitation, of video-cued discussions, 35
faculty and students, learning gap with, 126
families, 42; origins of, 47; and schools, in urban settings, 56
Family, School, and Community course, 18, 53, 54; community guest speakers with, 56–57; community of learners project with, 56, 57; instructional background about families and schools in urban settings, 56
Family Immigration Story Project, 41; ECE student teachers with, 41–48; first-generation immigrant or child of first-generation immigrants with, 43–44;

project guidelines for, 43–44, 49; project implementation, 44; PSTs engaged with power of story, 42–43; reflections, 45–48; story gathering, 44, 44–45
Family-School Collaboration Plan, 44
feedback, 13, 25
field-based opportunities, for tech-savvy teachers, 132
field trip, with PLCs, 80
fieldwork, 4–5, 14
final exam, for mathematics assessment: guidelines for, 99–100; topics for, 102
Finley, Ron, 93
first-generation immigrants, 43–44
Fleming, Denise, 79
food equity, 93
formative feedback, 25
foundations. *See* preservice teachers, course in foundations and pedagogy for
fractions, 102, 105–106
Fred Rogers Center for Early Learning and Children's Media, at Saint Vincent College, 131
friends, working, with "Six Object Task" activity, 115–116
fun and play connection, with "Six Object Task" activity, 111
functionality, of iPads, 129
Funds of Knowledge, 118

gender, 138–139
goals, 20, 76
The Great Teacher's Teach Off (GTTO), 91–92
The Green Machine (Ritz), 93
group norms challenged, by "Six Object Task" activity, 114–115
group project, for Activity Plan Simulations, 6–7
GTTO. *See* The Great Teacher's Teach Off
guest speakers, 22, 56–57
guidelines: for assignments, 68–70; for exploration of impactful practices, vii–viii; for Family Immigration Story Project, 43–44, 49; for mathematics assessment, 99–100
Guzzi, Bella, 17

hands-on activities, 57–59
"Head, Shoulders, Knees, and Toes", 59
HES. *See* Hopewell Elementary School
high-quality partners, for tech-savvy teachers, 128, 131–132, 133–134
Hopewell Elementary School (HES), 90
hydroponic gardens: basic and benefits of, 88; discovery with, 92; experiential learning with, 92; flexibility of, 88; at HES, 90; implementation of, 90–94; lessons learned with, 94–95; nature-based learning, 87–88, 94; vertical, 90
hygge, 66
"I Like Myself" (Beaumont), 59

immigration, 34–35; journeys relating to, 45–46. *See also* Family Immigration Story Project
impactful practices, 13; of community of learners, 52–57; of cultural beliefs visibility, in early childhood teacher education, 32–33; definition of, viii–ix; framing of, viii; guidelines for exploration of, vii–viii; of iPad integration, 126; for mathematics assessment, 97, 99; for online teacher education, 137, 145; of "Six Object Task" activity, 111, 112; teacher educators use of, vii, viii, ix, x, 52–54, 56
improvisational performance-based learning experience, 19
in-class discussions, 58–59
innovation, in curriculum and instruction, x–xi
instruction: classroom, 5–6; innovation in, x–xi
instructors, modeling of, viii
InTASC. *See* Interstate Teacher Assessment and Support Consortium
Integrated Curriculum, 53, 54; antibias curriculum, 55–56; DAP relating to, 55–56
integrated studies, with PLCs, 78–79
interactions, 5, 17–19; with PLCs, 77
interdependent team work, with PLCs, 80
International Society for Technology in Education (ISTE) standards, 127, 128

Interstate Teacher Assessment and Support Consortium (InTASC), viii
Introduction to Multicultural Education, 138
invented strategies, for mathematics, 102, 103, 104
iPads, 125–126, 127–129
ISTE. *See* International Society for Technology in Education

Japanese preschool teacher example, 36–37
journeys: immigration, 45–46; of pattern of practice, 63
joy of profession, embracing of, 70–71

kindergarten, 53

language, 7–8; support of, 10, 14
Leaf Man (Ehlert), 78
learning, 63, 64, 65–66, 67; active strategies for, 67; collaborative teams for, 75–76; documentation for, 68–70; experience of, 18, 19, 126; gap with, 126; technology infrastructure objectives for, 129, 130–131
learning community, 67–68. *See also* community of learners; professional learning communities
Likert Scale, 78
limited experience, of PSTs, 3–4
literacy, with technology infrastructure, 129–130
love, 53

mathematics: algorithms, 102, 103, 105; fractions, 102, 105–106; invented strategies for, 102, 103, 104; low self-efficacy with, 97; negative views of, 97; oral final for, 98, 106–108; understanding and methodology of, 97, 98, 106
mathematics assessment, 97–99; lessons learned about, 106–108; scores for, 103–104; signupgenius.com, 101; of students, 103–104; study sessions with, 101
mathematics assessment implementation, 99, 101, 103–104; considerations prior to, 100–102; final exam guidelines with, 99–100; final exam topics with, 102; sample questions for, 104–106; success of, 102–103; time commitment for, 100–101
Mendler, Allen, 21
mentors, for tech-savvy teachers, 131, 132
models, 92, 93–94, 129; demonstrations to, viii, 9–10, 13, 57–58; for preservice/in-service teachers, 63–64; for teacher educators, 63
monocultural approaches, 47
motivation, with "Six Object Task" activity, 111
multicultural education course, 138–139
multicultural perspectives, with community of learners, 53–54, 55
multilingual children, 47
multimedia applications, of iPads, 127–128
multi-voice approach, 52
Musselwhite, Helen, 79
mutual accountability, 76

NAAEE. *See* North American Association for Environmental Education
National Association for the Education of Young Children (NAEYC), viii, 13, 55, 65, 131
National Science Teachers Association, 88
Natural Start Alliance, 87
nature-based learning, with hydroponic gardens, 87–88, 94
negative views, of mathematics, 97
"New Jersey School District Eases Pressure on Students, Baring and Ethnic Divide" (Spencer), 34
nontraditional learners, online teacher education for, 137
normative, culture- and value-free classroom practices, 32
North American Association for Environmental Education (NAAEE), 87
nurturance, 53
nutrition, 93

One Minute Read, 129–130
online class presentation assignment, 140–141

online resources, for pseudo-conferences, 20–22
online teacher education, 137; chat rooms for, 143–144; connections with, 145; impactful practices for, 137, 145; lessons learned about, 142–143; for nontraditional learners, 137; online web meetings for, 144; pedagogy relating to, 137; in sources of diversity, 137
online teacher education, for collaborative skills, 137, 140; online class presentation assignment, 140–141; for technology comfortable candidates, 141
online teacher education, for culturally responsive teachers, 137–138; about bias, 138, 139; about class, 138, 139; about culture, 138; about ethnic diversity, 138; about gender, 138–139; with multicultural education course, 138–139; about prejudice, 138; about race, 138–139; about sexism, 139; student diversity relating to, 138; about white dominion, 139
online teacher education, for technology skilled teachers, 137, 139; podcast assignment, 139–140; technical pedagogy relating to, 139; web page assignment, 140
online web meetings, 144
open-ended design and redesign, with "Six Object Task" activity, 113–115; complex and collaborative, 115–117
oral final, for mathematics, 98, 106–108

parent and student relationships, 17–18
parent panels, 18, 19, 22; discussions for, 22–23; guest speakers for, 22
parent-teacher conference, 19, 20, 23–24
pattern of practice: definition of, 63–65; impact of, 64; journey of, 63; lessons learned, 72–73; as model for preservice/in-service teachers, 63–64; as model for teacher educators, 63; NAEYC relating to, 65; outcomes linked to, 71–72; playful learning with, 63, 64; recommended resources for, 73; six elements of, 63–64; for teacher educator, 63, 64, 67, 70, 71–73

pattern of practice implementation, 64, 65; with active learning strategies, 67; with class historian assignment guidelines, 68–70; engaging with course material, 67; with explorations beyond classroom, 67–68; first day, 65–66; invitation to learning, 65–66; joy of profession embraced, 70–71; last day, 70–71; learning community extended, 67–68; learning documented, 68–70; positive rapport with, 66; reflective practice engagement, 71, 72–73
pedagogy, 14, 55, 121; exceptional children relating to, 4–6, 11, 14; iPads relating to, 128; online teacher education relating to, 137; of play, with Project Zero, 64, 66; technical, 139
personal cultural identity, 47
physical disabilities, 11, 12
play-based teaching practice, 119
playful learning, 63, 64
PLCs. *See* professional learning communities
PLTs. *See* Professional Learning Teams
podcast assignment, 139–140
positive rapport, 66
PowerPoint (PPT) presentation, 140–141, 143
practice document, parent-teacher conference, 19, 20
practices, 13, 14; alignment of standards and, 127; best, vii, 35–36; culturally based child rearing, 11; DAP, 55–56; effective, vii, 75–76; normative, culture- and value-free classroom, 32; play-based teaching, 119; reflective practice engagement, 71, 72–73; shared, vii. *See also* impactful practices; pattern of practice; pattern of practice implementation
pragmatics, activity plan simulators relating to, 8
pre-course survey, with PLCs, 76–77
prejudice, 138
preschool, 53
Preschool in Three Cultures Revisited, 33, 35
presentations: with Activity Plan Simulations, 7, 13–14; with Family

Immigration Story Project, 46–48; PowerPoint, 140–141, 143
preservice teachers (PSTs): competencies for, 3, 6, 13; development of, 13–14; limited experience of, 3–4; PLCs for, 75–76, 77, 80–82; power of story engaged by, 42–43; self-reflection of, 36, 51; strengths-based framework used by, 4; transition of, 75
preservice teachers, community of learners created for, 51–52; discussions relating to, 53–54; Family, School, and Community course for, 18, 53, 54, 56–57; Integrated Curriculum course for, 53, 54–56; teacher educator help with, 52–54, 56
preservice teachers, course in foundations and pedagogy for, 4; classroom instruction with, 5–6; at community college, 4–6; discussions with, 5; fieldwork with, 4–5, 14; interaction with, 5; observations with, 5, 11
professional-academic language, 7–8
professional development opportunities, for tech-savvy teachers, 131–132
professional learning communities (PLCs): collaborative learning teams as, 75–76; common goals with, 76; definition of, 76; effective practices promoted by, 75–76; mutual accountability with, 76; for PSTs, 75–76, 77, 80–82
professional learning communities (PLCs), implementation of, 76; with assignments, 78; challenges with, 81–82; with clinical field experience, 79–80; with discussions, 80–81; with field trip, 80; with foundation of knowledge, 77; with integrated studies, 78–79; with interactions, 77; with interdependent team work, 80; with pre-course survey, 76–77; with strategies, 77–78; with team score, 80
Professional Learning Teams (PLTs), 77, 81, 82
professorial support, for Activity Plan Simulations, 7–11, 13, 14
proficiency, with technological infrastructure, 126
progressions, viii

progressive theorists, 118
Project Zero, pedagogy of play of, 64, 66
pseudo-conferences, 18, 19, 23–24; as improvisational performance-based learning experience, 19; online resources for, 20–22; parent-teacher conference practice document for, 19, 20; preparation for, 19–22; websites for, 20–22
pseudo-parent-teacher conference, 23; context of, 23; student profiles for, 23–24
PST. *See* preservice teachers

race, 51, 138–139
reflective practice, 13, 14
reflective practice engagement, 71, 72–73
relational engagement, 51
relational positionality, 36, 37
relationships: changes in, 45–46, parent and student, 17–18; teacher and family, 42
"Rethinking Difficult Parents" (Mendler), 21
Ritz, Stephen, 93
role-play, 9, 10, 11–12, 14

sample questions, for mathematics assessment, 104–106
Sánchez, Sylvia, 43
scaffolding, 54, 55, 64
scores, for mathematics assessment, 103–104
seeing and hearing each other online is important, 142
self, sense of, 41
self-culturalectomy, 32
self-efficacy, 14, 97
self-evaluation, 78, 81
self-reflection, 36, 51
sensitivity, importance of, 39
sexism, 139
shared power, collaboration through, 42
signupgenius.com, 101
"Six Object Task" activity: benefits of, 111; composition of, 117; conclusion to, 122; for ECE teacher preparation, 111; example of, 121; fun and play connection with, 111; impactful

practice of, 111, 112; motivation with, 111; usefulness of, 111

"Six Object Task" activity, debrief process with, 117; creativity fostered during, 120; ECE STEM/STEAM education, 117, 120–122; play-based teaching practice, 119

"Six Object Task" activity, implementation of: complex and collaborative open-ended design and redesign with, 115–117; conduction of, 113–117; connections with, 115, 118; friends working with, 115–116; group norms challenged with, 114–115; open-ended design and redesign with, 113–115; stage setting for, 112–113; teams working with, 116–117

small-group activities, 8–9, 14

social-emotional teaching and learning, with hydroponic gardens, 93–94

social justice, 55

Spencer, Kyle, 34

stage setting, for "Six Object Task" activity, 112–113

standards and practices, alignment of, 127

STEAM. *See* ECE STEM/STEAM education

STEM. *See* ECE STEM/STEAM education

story gathering: with immigration journeys, 45–46; reflections on, 44, 44–45; with relationship changes, 45–46; repeated themes with, 45–46

strengths-based framework, PSTs use of, 4

student and parent relationship, creating voice with, 17–18

student-led inquiry, with hydroponic gardens, 92

student profiles, 19, 23–24, 27–29

students, 126, 138; with disabilities, iPads for, 128–129; diverse population, of students, 51–52, 53, 54, 138; mathematics assessment of, 103–104

students into teachers, transformation of, viii–ix

student teachers. *See* early childhood education

study sessions, for mathematics assessment, 101

tablets, 125–126

teacher candidates engaged in culture conversations, 36; concerns relating to, 36; cultural appropriateness relating to, 37; emotional responses relating to, 36, 47; about Japanese preschool teacher example, 36–37

teachercomplaints.com, 21

teacher course, for exceptional children, 4–6, 11, 14

teacher education. *See* online teacher education

teacher educators, 41, 48, 75; coevalness and, 52; of color, 54; cultural beliefs relating to, 33, 34–35, 37, 39; impactful practices used by, vii, viii, ix, x; model for, 63; pattern of practice for, 63, 64, 67, 70, 71–73; relational engagement taught by, 51; worldviews of, 54. *See also* cultural beliefs visibility, in early childhood teacher education

teacher educators, community of learners relating to: impactful practices with, 52–54, 56; implementation of, 57–59

teachers: cultural experiences of, 31–32; empathy of, 31–32; objectivity of, 32; relationships of family and, 42

teachhub.com, 21

teaching and learning, with hydroponic gardens, 90–91

"Teaching Early Childhood Mathematics", 98

teaching practice, play-based, 119

teaching workforce, diverse, 48

teams, 80, 81–82; for "Six Object Task" activity, 116–117; *See also specific teams*

technical pedagogy, 139

technological challenges, with technological infrastructure, 126, 127

technology, with iPads, 126, 128–129

technology comfortable candidates, online education for, 141

technology infrastructure, for tech-savvy teachers, 126

technology skilled teachers, 137, 139–140

tech-savvy teachers, 125–126, 127; challenges embraced by, 130–131; final thoughts about, 133–134; high-quality

Index

partners for, 128, 131–132, 133–134; ISTE standards for, 127, 128; lessons learned by, 132–133; tablets for, 125–126

tech-savvy teachers, high-quality partner for, 128, 131, 133–134 collaborative research opportunities relating to, 132; field-based opportunities relating to, 132; mentors as, 131, 132; professional development opportunities relating to, 131–132

tech-savvy teachers, iPads for, 125–126; in coursework, 127–129; digital storytelling with, 127–128; functionality of, 129; multimedia applications of, 127–128; technology with, 126, 128–129

tech-savvy teachers, technology infrastructure for, 126–127; appropriateness of, 130–131; collaborative workshop model with, 129; learning objectives for, 129, 130–131; literacy with, 129–130; methods for, 129–130

TED talk, 93

time commitment, for mathematics assessment, 100–101

Tobin, Joseph, 33, 34

tower gardens, 88, 89

training areas, with technological infrastructure, 126

transformation, of students into teachers, viii–ix

transformative education, 51

transformative experiences, 51, 53

transversal competence skills, 120

understanding and methodology, of mathematics, 97, 98, 106

usefulness, of "Six Object Task" activity, 111

vernacular language, 8

vertical hydroponic gardens, 90

video-cued discussions, 32, 33; benefits of, 34–35; best practices relating to, 35–36; case studies with, 34; facilitation of, 35; immigration relating to, 34–35; overview of, 33–34

voice, multi-voice approach to, 52. *See also* creating voice

Voice Thread, 142

A Walk Through the Woods (Musselwhite), 79

web page assignment, 140

websites, for pseudo-conferences, 20–22

What Goes Where? activity, 12

Where Once There Was a Wood (Fleming), 79

white dominion, 139

Zoom video conferencing, 141, 144

About the Editors and Contributors

Christopher J. Meidl, PhD. Meidl's pre-K–12 teaching experience includes public schools in Beloit, Wisconsin, New Orleans and Westwego, Louisiana, and La Joya, Texas. He has a master's in education degree in curriculum and instruction from the University of New Orleans and a doctorate in curriculum and instruction in early childhood education from The Pennsylvania State University. He currently teaches PK–4 courses at Duquesne University. His research and community engagement focus on character education, classroom management, white teachers and diverse communities, and black males in early childhood education. meidlc@duq.edu

Louise Ammentorp, PhD, is an associate professor in the Elementary and Early Childhood Education Department at The College of New Jersey. Her teaching and research focuses on enriching the clinical experiences of preservice teachers and best practices in teaching and learning, in particular nature and arts-based education, environmental sustainability education, and the use of hydroponic gardens in the classroom. ammentor@tcnj.edu

* * *

Alan Bates, PhD, is a professor of early childhood education at Illinois State University in the School of Teaching and Learning. He primarily teaches the math methods courses for early childhood majors and his research interests include children's mathematical development and teachers' math self-efficacy. He can be contacted at abates@ilstu.edu.

Billi L. Bromer, PhD, is an associate professor in the College of Education at Brenau University and the coordinator of teacher education at the university's regional campus in Augusta, Georgia. She is an active member of the national Association of Teacher Educators (ATE) and currently serves as the co-chair of the Early Childhood Teacher Educator Special Interest Group within ATE. Prior to becoming a teacher educator, Dr. Bromer was an early childhood special educator, providing collaborative consultation to teachers in Head Start, Georgia's pre-K program, and other early education settings. During that time, she also served on the Georgia Department of Education State Advisory Panel for Special Education. Dr. Bromer is an NAEYC/CAEP Specialized Professional Association reviewer.

Laurel L. Byrne, PhD, is an assistant professor of education at La Salle University. Dr. Byrne's work as an early childhood teacher educator at both the undergraduate and graduate levels inform her practice and research in the field of early childhood teacher preparation. byrneL@lasalle.edu

Leslie Craigo, PhD, is an assistant professor at Borough of Manhattan Community College (BMCC) in the Teacher Education Department. She teaches courses in child development, sociological foundations of early childhood education, foundation and pedagogy for exceptional children, and supervised fieldwork with infants and toddlers. Dr. Craigo is also a member of the advisory board of several childcare centers. She has authored several articles and presents at local and national conferences on areas related to teacher education, diversity, literacy, and special education. For 17 years prior to her appointment at BMCC, Dr. Craigo was a classroom teacher in various positions, from prekindergarten to grade three, in general education, special education, inclusive classrooms, collaborative team teaching, and self-contained special education classrooms. She was also a special educator for early intervention and an educational evaluator.

Alyse C. Hachey, PhD, is an associate professor, lead early childhood faculty member, and co-director of the College of Education Makerspace at the University of Texas at El Paso. Her teaching and research interests focus on early childhood cognition and curriculum development, particularly related to ECE STEM education.

Debra Hyatt-Burkhart, PhD, LPC, NCC, ACS, is an associate professor and director of program practices of the Counselor Education & Supervision program at Duquesne University. She has taught at the graduate and undergraduate levels, and has provided myriad trainings to community counseling agencies. Dr. Hyatt-Burkhart has published on issues related to positive approaches and responses to working with trauma; clinical supervision; and marriage, family, and couples counseling, and has presented internationally and nationally on these topics. She has an extensive background in community-based mental health practice, clinical supervision, and administration, with over 30 years of experience in the field.

MinSoo Kim-Bossard, PhD, received her PhD in curriculum and instruction (early childhood education) and comparative and international education from The Pennsylvania State University. Dr. Kim-Bossard's research and teaching combine the fields of educational anthropology, reconceptualist scholarship in early childhood education, and studio-based pedagogical practices borrowed from art education.

Lisa L. Minicozzi, EdD, is an assistant professor of early childhood education and program director for educational leadership in the College of Education and Health Sciences at Adelphi University. A former elementary school teacher and K–5 principal, Dr. Minicozzi values working with teacher candidates to prepare them for teaching in today's diverse and complex early childhood classrooms. She is an NYS Dignity for All Students Act trainer, who coaches a number of teaching professionals on how to create positive learning environments for all children. Her research interests include teaching early childhood special education, with a focus on the implications of innovative technologies such as the iPad for the special needs learner and how early childhood educators grapple with standards-based education and the pressures of accountability. lminicozzi@adelphi.edu

Rebecca J. Pruitt, PhD, is an associate professor in the Department of Educational Studies at Lewis University and director of early childhood special education. She holds a PhD in curriculum studies, a master's of science in family relations and child development, and a bachelor's of arts in early childhood. She can be reached at pruittre@lewisu.edu.

Jill A. Smith, PhD, is an assistant professor of education at Central Methodist University. She holds a PhD in curriculum and instruction from the University of Missouri. Jill has taught graduate and undergraduate courses in early childhood and elementary education at the University of Houston–Clear Lake and at Central Methodist University. jsmith@centralmethodist.edu

Julia Ann Williams, PhD, is an assistant professor and director of the pre-K–4 program in the School of Education at Duquesne University. She has over 30 years of experience in working with young children and families and over 25 years of experience in preparing preservice teachers. Her primary focus is to inform and educate preservice teachers to have an effective, positive impact on the social and emotional development of young children and to provide a classroom environment that appreciates and uplifts the varied lived experiences of children and families.

www.ingramcontent.com/pod-product-compliance
Lightning Source LLC
Chambersburg PA
CBHW021851300426
44115CB00005B/105